A Journey Through my memories....

SHOBHA SRIVASTAVA

BlueRose ONE
Stories Matter

BLUEROSE PUBLISHERS
India | U.K.

BlueRose ONE
Stories Matter

For permissions requests or inquiries regarding this publication, please contact:

BLUEROSE PUBLISHERS
www.BlueRoseONE.com
info@bluerosepublishers.com
+91 8882 898 898
+4407342408967

ISBN: 978-93-5819-538-5

Cover design: [Yash]
Typesetting: [Pooja Sharma]

First Edition: July 2023

Dedicated to my children

Manjari, Leena, Anubhav & my grandson Ayush

Prelude

Allow me to transport you through the corridors of time, as I pen down some cherished moments of my life. Inspired by the encouragement of my children, I have embarked on this journey of reminiscence, hoping to bring you joy through my words. It is a chance to relive my life once more, with the warmth of nostalgia.

I, Shobha Srivastava, took my first breath in the loving embrace of a traditional middle-class family, nestled in the town of Orai near Jhansi. Born in the year 1943, I was the second child among six siblings, my roots deeply intertwined with the land that bore the legendary Jhansi Ki Rani, Lakshmi Bai. I am of course proud to hail from a place steeped in valor and courage!

Immersed in the tale of my existence, I realize that my journey would have been incomplete without the presence of my beloved parents. My father, Ramakant Srivastava, hailing from a prominent Zamindar family, possessed an adventurous spirit. As an electrical engineer in the Central Railway, he embarked on a quest to explore the world beyond. My mother, Vidyavati Srivastava, a well-educated and skilled homemaker from Jhansi, enriched our lives with her nurturing presence and culinary expertise.

It is through the guidance and love of my remarkable parents that I have become the person I am today. They instilled in me the values of compassion and integrity, shaping my character. My father, a jovial soul with ambitious dreams for his children, strived to provide us with the best opportunities. As the eldest among my sisters, I was bestowed with special attention. During summer vacations, my father would enroll me in a number of classes, ranging from Kathak dance to singing, stitching, hand embroidery, machine embroidery (where our hand machine was ingeniously transformed into a foot-operated one), and even cooking lessons from a Bengali teacher, indulging my sweet tooth with delicious Bengali sweets.

From a young age, I found solace in the pages of books, and Mills & Boon novels became my teenage obsession, fueling my romantic heart. After completing my graduation from Ruia College, Bombay, I pursued a Master's degree in Applied Psychology from Jabalpur. Amidst the many activities in life, painting and music emerged as my cherished hobbies, offering solace and joy during my leisure hours.

Growing up amidst the bustling city life of Bombay, I also had the privilege of experiencing the idyllic charm of my paternal house in the village of Ladgawa. The memories of village life remain vivid and treasured, forever etched in my mind.

As the years unfolded, my husband Rajesh and I embarked on a remarkable journey, celebrating 59 years of togetherness. Life led us through a myriad of experiences, traversing different places as we navigated the ever-changing tides of his career. Through the ups and downs, we stood by each other's side, finding solace in both joyous and challenging moments. Our bickering and nagging only served to strengthen our bond, a testament to the enduring love we share.

We witnessed the transformation of eras, from the bioscope to YouTube, from handwritten letters to mobile phones, and from letters to iPads. Life bestowed upon us a delightful interplay of fun and frolic, surpassing any expectations we had. We are truly grateful for the blessings life has bestowed upon us.

Our family expanded to include three children and a precious grandchild, each entering our lives in different phases, bringing immense joy and shaping our experiences. They have made us laugh and cry, providing invaluable life lessons. All of them have achieved remarkable success in their respective fields, becoming a source of immense pride. Money may bring material wealth, but it is our children who have enriched our lives beyond measure, offering the truest form of richness.

My eldest daughter, Manjari (Cuckoo), has flourished as a professor in a college, holding an MBA in Marketing and Computers and recently completing her PhD. The second, Dr. Leena, has embraced her passion as one of the few Developmental Pediatricians in the country after her specialization in that field. My son, Anubhav (Mintoo), a banker, pursued an MBA from IIM Lucknow and now serves in ICICI Bank. Our grandchild, Ayush got a Master's degree from the US and is now working there. This is our immediate family, a treasure trove that has brought immeasurable happiness.

As social beings, the fabric of our lives also includes friendships and relationships within society. While friendships hold a special place, it is our family that truly shines as the greatest jewel in our lives.

It is essential to flow with the rhythm of time, for stagnant waters breed discontent. Moreover, the journey of life is a continuous learning process, with lessons that surpass what no school can impart.

In the midst of it all, we must remember that self-care is of utmost importance. Nurturing our bodies and minds and finding happiness in the little things may sound like mere preaching. Yet, in the face of life's challenges, we should never lose hope or give up. Embracing a positive mindset and cherishing life's simple pleasures allows us to truly savor the beauty that surrounds us.

Shobha Srivastava June 2, 2023

As I think about my life, it is crucial to delve into the roots that define my being. Here is a brief overview of my family tree, divided into chapters that shape my story.

On my paternal side, my grandfather, Meva Lal Srivastava, affectionately known as Baba, was a Zamindar in the village of Ladgawa, Fatehpur and lived with my grandmother Girija Devi. My father, Ramakant, was one of four brothers, namely Laxmikant, Krishnakant, and Bishunkant, and had three sisters: Hemlata, Prem Late, and Om Lata.

Turning to my maternal lineage, my grandmother, Nani Pan Kunwar Bai, and my late grandfather, Nana Shitala Sahay Srivastava, played significant roles in shaping my mother's life. Sadly, my mother lost her father at the tender age of one. Yet, Nani's brother Thakur Prasad Srivastava, stood as a pillar of support, aiding her journey towards independence by helping her become a teacher. Alongside them, my mother shared a close bond with her cousins, such as Shanta Mausi, Prema Mausi, Rajjan Mama, and Baby Mama, who were like family to us, always there for my mother.

Within my immediate family, my father, Ramakant, and my mother, Vidyavati, nurtured the foundation of love and togetherness. My siblings and their spouses are as follows:

1. Eldest Brother: Sushil and Madhu, blessed with two children, Roopesh and Neetu.

2. Myself: Shobha and my husband Rajesh, with our children Manjari, Leena, Anubhav, and grandson Ayush.
3. Sister: Bina and her husband Ajay, parents of Sameer and Sumit.
4. Sister: Usha and her husband Prem, with their children Priya, Deepika, and Parsoon.
5. Brother: Harish and his wife Manjula and their children Mili and Hitesh.
6. Brother: Anoop and his wife Reeta, parents to Neha and Anurag.

This serves as a brief depiction of my beloved family, each member weaving their unique threads into the fabric of our lives and forming a fabric of love, support, and cherished memories.

Contents

PART 1

The Formative Years – 1943 To 1953 at Jhansi

Immerse yourself in the nostalgic scene of a lively 10-year-old girl, frolicking in a vibrant printed frock with two neatly braided hair adorned with cheerful red ribbons. That girl is me, Shobha, a name resonating with youthful innocence and joy. I affectionately referred to my parents as Amma and Baboo, and my elder brother Sushil as Bade Bhaiya.

Our journey begins in the city of Jhansi, Uttar Pradesh, where my parents tied the knot in 1940 before embarking on their new life together. Settling in the quaint neighborhood of Kishan Singh Ka Mohalla, Sipri Bazar, we called a small yellow house our home. It housed a cozy living room, two modest bedrooms, a kitchen, and a charming courtyard. Ascending the staircase from the courtyard led to the rooftop terrace, adorned with a small room—our study den during the day and a sleeping haven at night. In the scorching summers, we eagerly sought refuge under the starry sky, relishing the cool breeze atop the terrace. To combat the unforgiving climate, we sprinkled water on the cots in the evening, preparing them for a refreshing night's sleep.

The bustling aangan, our backyard, served as the gateway for Mehari (our domestic help), the friendly mahajin (local grocer), and our diligent sweeper. A pair of traditional Indian toilets stood at one end, while a tap and a charming chabutra adorned the other side. Our daily water supply relied on the presence of five or six large drums, carefully filled to quench our thirst and meet our household needs. In one corner, a pile of wooden planks and coal awaited their turn on the sigdi and chulha, for cooking mouthwatering delicacies. A grand brass vessel and a humble earthen mataka housed our drinking water, ensuring its purity and refreshing taste.

When it was time to dine, we gathered around and ate from kansa thalis and katoris, savoring every morsel of our meals. For us children, petite and enchanting thalis awaited, inviting us to sit cross-legged on wooden planks adorning the floor. This vivid portrayal offers a mere glimpse into the inner sanctum of our humble abode, where love, simplicity, and cherished memories resonated within each nook and corner.

In front of our house, there was a large space where children could play. In the veranda, our only vehicle, a cycle with a bell, stood. Baboo used it to go to work.

As I mentioned before, we were six siblings. The oldest was Sushil, followed by me, then Bina, Usha, Harish, and Anoop, who was added to the family just two months ago. Over a span of ten years, from 1941 to 1953, we came into the world with a two-year gap between each of us, except for Anoop, who arrived three years after Harish.

Whenever there was a new addition to the family, our nani (maternal grandmother) would come and stay with us for at least two months. She would take care of Amma, the newborn child, and us. Nani was a primary school teacher in Konch, a place near Orai, but she always spent her summer vacations with us. We were always delighted when she visited because she would bring a variety of delicious treats like mithai, sattu, laddu, buknu, and many potalies (bags) of bajra atta, birchun, aam papad, and a big tin of pure ghee. Nani was a strong, hefty lady with good height.

She would make different kinds of laddoos for Amma, made from sonth, gondh, turmeric, and dry fruits, to be eaten after delivery. For us, she would create guddi and gudda (dolls) from old clothes and dress them up in nice outfits. We girls used to play with the dolls, get them married, and have fun.

From morning onwards, our house buzzed with activities. We went to school, Baboo went to work, and everyone's dabba and breakfast needed to be prepared. We children often fought with each other, especially my brother Sushil who enjoyed teasing us. Amma would shout at us. I forgot to mention that our cousin, Prakash Bhaisaab, also stayed with us because he got a job here.

I don't know how Amma managed to handle everything, but ladies are always multitaskers. In addition to her responsibilities, she also took care of our studies. There was no KG or nursery at that time, so Amma and Nani would teach us using a slate and chalk. We were directly admitted to first or second grade, and no birth certificates were required. Prakash Bhaisaab acted as our guardian for school matters and even styled our hair in the morning, making a choti (braided hair) for me as I had long hair and Amma had too much work to do.

Our school was within a 10-minute walking distance. Our immediate neighbor was a Bengali family, the Chatterjis. They had a daughter named Deepa, whom we affectionately called Deepa Didi. Another family, the Varmas, lived in front of our house, and their children were around the same age as us. Both families were close family friends, and we would often visit each other.

On our way to school, there was a Gurudwara and a big red letterbox, which served as the primary means of communication at that time. We remember the Gurudwara more vividly because we used to go there for kada prasad and enjoy it. Sundays were especially fun because Baboo had a sweet tooth. He would buy hot jalebis in a big dona (vessel made out of leaves) from a nearby halwai and we would have milk and jalebis for breakfast. Occasionally, he would also buy Kewal Halwai pedha, which was another favorite sweet dish. Recently, my elder brother went to Jhansi and visited the same shop, but he found the taste not as delightful, realizing that memories are often sweeter.

Another interesting thing we did was visiting Amma's uncle's house on all festivals. He was Amma's father's brother, and he treated Amma no less than his own daughter. On festivals, they would give saris to Amma and money to all the children. We would get excited as we dressed up in nice clothes and went on a tonga (horse-drawn carriage) ride, enjoying festive foods like puri, kachori, and kheer. There were three maternal uncles and one maternal aunt, Amma's cousins: Rajjan Mama, Baby Mama, Ravi Mama, and Indu Mausi. Indu Mausi was two or three years older than me, as far as I can recall. All the maternal uncles were talented singers, and one of them played the harmonium, while Mausi danced to their music. One of my cousins, the son of one of the uncles, even played the flute. It was a musically gifted family.

Their house was a double-story building, and at the back, there was a bawadi, a type of pond with steps on all sides. It was quite deep, and we would sit on the steps and watch our uncles swim in different styles. I don't think they had any swimming coach or music master; they seemed to be naturally gifted. Many other cousins of Amma would also visit in the evening. There was a strong sense of family bonding during those times. In the evenings, we would bid farewell with hugs from the elders and touch their feet as a sign of respect, with kisses often planted on children's foreheads or cheeks.

There is one interesting incident that Amma used to narrate often, about the time when I was 5 or 6 years old and skipped school to play kancha (a game involving marbles) with the neighboring children. I didn't go to school for a day or two, and my older brother and I had similar school bags. One day, I mistakenly took his school bag. When he opened the bag in class and found it was mine, he came and informed Nani (grandmother), as Harish, my younger brother, was born during that time. Nani was in charge of the house, and she scolded me. Being a teacher herself, she was strict about discipline. However, one thing she taught us was to always share whatever we ate with our siblings. Being the elder siblings, my older brother and I learned many valuable lessons from her.

Many relatives used to visit during that time, and we would often go to visit the famous Jhansi Ka Killa (Jhansi Fort). I also went with them once or twice, but I found it boring back then.

The days were passing by, and suddenly one day there was commotion in Amma's room. Both parents were discussing something. Later, we came to know that Baboo had been promoted and transferred to Bombay. We were excited because Baboo had to join his new position within a fortnight. He went, and our packing began as well.

When I look back now, 1953 was a year of change for us. After three months, Baboo got a railway quarter in Parel. He came back, and our furniture was packed and sent by a luggage bogie provided by the railways. When we were traveling to Bombay, we had two or three big steel trunks and two holdalls. We also carried a large steel tiffin carrier with four compartments and a surahi, an earthen long-necked pot in a wooden stand that always accompanied us for cold water. During the long journey, the surahi had to be filled at different stations.

Baboo was very punctual, and our luggage was put in three or four tongas. We reached the station before time, as always, and were told to sit and wait in the waiting room. Baboo used to get a pass for the first class, so the first-class waiting room was huge, like all other structures from the British times. It was a large room with two big armchairs, a big table with a big mirror, benches, and other chairs. There was a round dining table and a big Indian fan, a type of curtain, on the ceiling that was moved by a man. Sometimes we children could play, running around and even play tabla on the dining table, as it was not crowded.

Jhansi was a big railway junction, and some office people of Baboo and our Mamaji were there to see us off. Finally, with the shrilling voice of the engine whistle, the train arrived. Our compartment with six berths was already reserved, so the luggage was pushed in by coolies and set in proper order. I ran and caught the window seat as I liked to count trees and water puddles as the train moved. Bade Bhaiya would be on the other window seat. After some time, it was lunchtime, and the tiffin carrier was opened. It contained lunch, dinner, and even breakfast. The smell of puri bhaji filled the bogie along with the aroma of homemade achar, which tasted even better during the journey. After some time in the afternoon, we took a nap. Two children shared one berth, with their heads on opposite sides.

A day and night passed. In between, Baboo bought some gulab jamuns in a big dona, along with tea and some of our favorite snacks from different stations. We passed the time singing, playing, and enjoying ourselves. The next morning, we brushed our teeth one by one in the moving train, enjoying the experience. Then we had breakfast of kachori and chai served in kulhads, bought by Baboo at some big station. Finally, we were about to reach Bombay.

PART 2

Growing Up In a Metro - 1954 To 1962 at Mumbai

Finally, our train was reaching Bombay, the city of dreams, Victoria Terminus now renamed as Chhatrapati Shivaji Terminus. Looking out of the window, I saw a band of red-turbaned coolies running towards the train as it slowed down. Even before the train had fully stopped, they entered the compartment and started pulling out the luggage. Baboo told all of us to get down and stay in one place. I was amazed to see a sea of people, all pushing and hurrying, running here and there. Meanwhile, Baboo must have hired coolies, so a cart arrived to load the luggage, and the coolies started carrying it. In a few minutes, we were running after them until we reached the taxi stand. I saw multi-storied tall buildings and huge film posters all around.

Meanwhile, two yellow and black taxis had been hired, and we sat in them, enjoying the view of the broad roads, buses, and trams. We reached our house in Parel. Since Baboo had already shifted, the house was ready. It was an old British-era construction, a big house with wooden partitions for rooms and a spacious kitchen. The kitchen had a standing-style platform with two "sigadis," which was very different from the kitchen in Jhansi. At the back of the house, there were some banana trees and a round iron staircase for going up, as it was a two-story house.

At the back, there was a servant quarter with a toilet for the servant. A bai (maid) was already there as Baboo had hired one in advance. This was a big relief for Amma as having a full-time servant was easier in Bombay, where finding a house was a big problem. A room with a toilet was a big asset, which made the availability of a maid at a cheaper rate easier.

From the next day onwards, we started settling in and getting acquainted with the neighbors. Since it was a railway colony, we children made friends within a few days. Amma also settled in with the new neighbors and the bai. The bai was very neat, clean, and efficient. Milk was delivered at our doorstep in glass bottles with blue lids. Here, there was no milkman, which was another change.

Then we started settling into school as well. Baboo had already admitted Bade Bhaiya and me to "Hindi High School" in Ghatkopar. Bina and Usha went to some nearby school, and Harish attended a railway convent school nearby.

Baboo, being a railway employee, arranged for us to have first-class railway passes as he was entitled to free passes for his family. We had to travel by local train from Parel to Ghatkopar. The railway station was about a 10-minute walk from our house. So both of us left the house at around 9 in the morning, after having a heavy breakfast, in our uniform (mine was a white blouse and a blue skirtwhich was more like a tunic). We carried our lunch boxes (dabba) and returned home around 4 or 5 in the evening.

At Ghatkopar, the school was very near the railway station. The school campus was quite big, with a three-floor building and a large ground for sports. It was a co-educational school, but boys and girls sat in different rows. I adjusted well to the new school soon, but since we joined in the middle of the session, I had to work hard in my studies in the first year. Here, there was good exposure to sports and games, which I loved. In the coming years, I made a place for myself in the kho kho and langadi teams as well. We were also taught Lazim and lathi fight during the physical training period and performed them during the Republic Day parade.

When we were in the 9th grade, I think we were taken for rifle training near our school, to a hilly area, to learn rifle shooting once a week. We were taught how to hold a rifle and how to aim through the hole, and basic training was given. Later on, it became a special training course for those who were interested and wanted to opt for it. I only learned that much, but it was a good experience. At that time, there was so much open space on the hill near our school and a nice view of the ghats. Now, the whole of Ghatkopar is full of buildings.

During Republic Day and Independence Day celebrations, there was great excitement in the air, accompanied by a strong sense of patriotism. Many children recited patriotic poems and sang songs. One girl would dress up as Bharat Mata, wearing a sari, with her hair open, holding a flag, and wearing a tiara made of cardboard on her head. The theme of national unity was highlighted in plays and skits that were performed, and the slogan "Bharat Mata ki jai" was frequently chanted. One of the participants always sang my favorite poem by Subhadra Kumari Chauhan, "Khub ladi mardani woh toh Jhansi wali Rani thi," which held special meaning for me as I spent my childhood in Jhansi. Another popular song was "Sare Jahan se achha Hindustan hamara."

When we were new to Bombay (now Mumbai), we used to go out at night to watch the city lights while sitting in trams and buses on Republic Day. The city would be beautifully illuminated, creating a mesmerizing sight. However, nowadays, the city remains lit up 24 hours a day.

Even within our house, changes were taking place. Baboo hired two carpenter brothers, Pandu and Damu, to make furniture for us. The furniture was crafted in one room, starting with a sofa, then a dining table, and eventually beds. A large table with a mirror and several drawers was made for us, with each of us having our own drawer to store our clothes. The furniture was expertly designed by Baboo, and I particularly loved the study table he made for me and my older brother, which had multiple drawers and was beautifully crafted. Some of the furniture still remains at my older brother's place to this day.

That reminds me, as soon as we moved into our new home, Baboo took us to a studio to have our photographs taken. We framed one photograph of all of us and hung it in the drawing room. Additionally, my mother's cross-stitch embroidery was framed and displayed in the dining room (as she used to create beautiful cross-stitch pieces). I still have some of her embroidery books, which I have fully utilized as I also enjoy cross-stitching. We adorned the walls with more family photographs and various pictures of Baboo, with him in the hockey team. All of these decorations made our new home feel warm and personal in just a few days.

Family Photo at the Studio in Bombay (sitting first from right)

Meanwhile, we also went for sightseeing on weekends to various places. As children, we particularly enjoyed visiting the zoo, aquarium, and the famous shoe-shaped structure called Kamla Nehru Park. We also indulged in delicious bhelpuri at Chowpatty Beach, and visited the Aarey Milk Colony, where we witnessed the mechanized process of filling milk bottles and savored the chilled sweet pink milk in small bottles, which became our favorite treat. Another thrilling experience was riding the double-decker tram, which had a fare of just 2 paisa at that time.

Juhu Beach held a special place in Baboo's heart, and we often went there for picnics. We would pack snacks, bread, bananas (which Baboo loved), and a dari to sit on. We would spread the mat under the shade of palm trees and enjoy the serene beach. During that time, it wasn't crowded at all. Amma would sit with my younger brother, Anoop, and gaze at the waves, observing the different moods of the sea. Meanwhile, the rest of us would run towards the sea. Baboo would teach all five of us how to face the tide, always showing great care and concern. My sisters and I would play with the sand, building houses by covering our feet with sand and even creating windows. We would compete with each other, play, and sing the playful song, "Chidiya Chidiya Mera Ghar Bana De, Nahi To Tere Sare Ande Phod Dungi." It was such a joyful experience.

The location of our house was excellent as well. We had a dispensary nearby for medical needs, and Dr. Vaidya, whose daughter Asha was one of my best friends, was in charge there. For major medical issues, there was a large hospital in Byculla.

Behind our house was a well-maintained railway ground where professional runners would practice. Many important kabaddi matches were also held there, drawing large crowds. We would sometimes watch the matches from our backstairs. During the summer vacations, our colony's children formed a team. We would wake up at 6 am, call each other, and go to the park for jogging. I'm not sure how it started, but everyone was punctual. Uncle Naresh Chacha, who was also from our colony, would lead our march past parade and organize games for us. We had a great playtime and would return home feeling tired and hungry, enjoying a hearty breakfast. This routine continued during all the holidays throughout our school days.

Nearby, there was a large railway club where we would go on weekends. The club had various games like table tennis, billiards, badminton, and volleyball, providing endless entertainment. I can't forget to mention the boxing room, where we watched many boxing matches. Boxer Buddy D'souza was a sensation during that time, and as teenagers, we were his biggest fans. We watched matches specifically because of him. He received the Arjuna Award in 1961.

The club also hosted occasional performances by famous orchestras, and a regular feature was the magic show. We were fortunate to witness many captivating performances by the renowned magician Senior P.C. Sircar in the club.

Baboo was a skilled bridge player and won many prizes in the game. He was a sports enthusiast, playing badminton, tennis, and hockey. My older brother Sushil also excelled in billiards.

There was an excellent library nearby, stocked with a vast collection of books and magazines, which captured my interest and ignited my love for reading. My first books were "Chandamama" and "Parag" as far as I remember. Then, for a long time, "Dharamyug" became my favorite magazine. It was quite large in size, and its editor, Dharmveer Bharati, was well-known. The magazine featured wonderful stories and even had a comic section along with some political news. During that time, I also read Hindi novels by authors like Gorapant, Shivani, and Premchand. "Illustrated Weekly of India" was also popular, and its editor, Khushwant Singh, was widely recognized. I started reading English novels after I joined college, but that library had an impressive collection of novels of all genres.

During the summer holidays, our Nani would arrive in Bombay, as she did every year, carrying two tin boxes filled with sattu, bajra atta, buknu, bari, and ladoo, along with a large can of pure ghee. She would travel alone from Orai to Bombay with these belongings, precious to us. Upon her arrival, the ghee would be heated in a big kadhai, and sendha salt was added as a preservative before storing it in large chini mitti jars. Amma and Nani would also prepare sweet and salty pickles of mangoes and raw jackfruit using fresh spices, mustard oil, and vinegar. Mustard oil was commonly used for cooking, except for sweet dishes, puris, and parathas, which were made with pure ghee.

I still remember the delicious meals we would have when coming home from school, hungry and eager to eat. Parathas or rotis with generous amounts of ghee, sprinkled with sugar or gud, ghee rotis with buknu, or mashed rotis soaked in milk or sattu with milk were our go-to options. Amma would also prepare a special sweet dish called "malida" using leftover bajra rotis in winter. The rotis would be mashed into small pieces, heated, and mixed with mashed gudd and lots of ghee.

During our vacation, we had the opportunity to taste Bombay's famous hapus mango for the first time, along with various types of pav, including hard, soft, and sweet buns. Red bananas and elaichi bananas were also a new and delightful experience. Additionally, pomfret fish became a natural choice instead of mutton for our weekend meals.

As our vacation neared its end, Baboo took the four of us to shop for rainy shoes and raincoats. Trying on raincoats with caps in the shop seemed amusingly funny, but once the rain came, we understood their practical use. We also purchased new books, copies, and other essentials for the upcoming school year. With each passing year, we became more adept at navigating local transportation.

During those days, we would receive a pocket money of 2 rupees. Outside our school, there were stalls selling ragda patties and ice golas, which cost one anna and 2 paisa. Ice gola was my personal favorite. On our way back from school, feeling hungry, we would buy channa and sangdana (mungphali or groundnuts) pudia for just 2 paisa. And of course, I can't forget the joy of indulging in a chocobar ice cream treat, courtesy of my friend Kusum, who had a generous pocket money allowance.

Most of my friends in school were Punjabi. There were a few who were older than me, including a girl named Santosh, who was quite plump. The classmates would tease her by saying, "Kis chakki ka atta khati ho" (Which flour mill do you eat from?). They would also share stories about how their education was affected by the partition. Over the years, I gradually started understanding Punjabi. They even taught me crochet needlework during school breaks, and we would gossip and make petticoat laces, which was a popular trend at the time. I later created many tablecloths with animal designs using those skills.

Gujarati was a compulsory subject from 5th to 11th grade, so I also learned to read and write Gujarati in school. Our school organized trips and picnics, taking us to places like Vasai Fort, Basin ka Killa, Kanheri Caves, and Elephanta Caves. We often visited Vihar Lake for picnics, as there was a shortcut from our school that involved walking through lanes of large water pipes. Sometimes we even walked on the water pipes, which added an adventurous touch to the experience.

Undoubtedly, everyone in Bombay must have their own memorable story about the rainy season. Let me share one of mine here.

It had been raining heavily since the previous day, so when I arrived at Ghatkopar local station after school, I learned that the local trains had stopped due to the rain. Bade Bhaiya, Sushil, had taken the previous train, and I was left stranded with a few other students. Fortunately, some teachers were also present, and they took us back to school. We stayed there for about 3 to 4 hours until a railway engine arrived and took us to Kurla station. From there, the local trains were running, and I finally reached Parel late at night. Baboo was waiting for me, and later, Amma told me that he had been anxiously going back and forth as there was no communication at the time. Bade bhaiya received a good scolding for leaving me and coming home without ensuring my safety. Now, as a parent, I can understand the worry and anxiety they must have experienced.

But life never stops in Bombay. Many of my classmates would come from Kalyan and Thane since there were fewer Hindi medium schools available. Sometimes they would even say that due to waterlogging, they had to travel by boat for part of the way. But regardless of the circumstances, everyone would make an effort to attend school during the rainy season.

On the home front, we had a great time as we used to celebrate numerous festivals throughout the year. Each festival was associated with different types of food, providing a variety of culinary delights throughout the year. Allow me to take a stroll down memory lane and share the festivals I remember.

First comes Nag Panchami, a festival where snakes are worshipped. Snake charmers would arrive in the morning and sit, showcasing their talent. They would take out snakes (with their venom supposedly removed) from their toknis (baskets) and feed them with milk provided by housewives. As children, we were filled with joy and amazement watching the spectacle. We would also give some money to the snake charmer. On that day, a simple lunch of channa, puri, and kheer would be prepared. It was believed that no vegetables should be cut or cooked on that day.

Next is Raksha Bandhan, which is still celebrated but with more flair. Nowadays, rakhis are often sent by courier, but back then, the postman would deliver them. During that time, postmen held significant importance as they would bring not only rakhis but also money orders, telegrams, and letters.

Following that is Krishna Janmashtami, which was always celebrated grandly in our house. We would observe a fast but would enjoy a variety of tasty dishes permitted during fasts, including makhana kheer, kuttu aata puri, potato and arbi bhaji, sakarkand halwa, and even salty makhana. We loved Janmashtami for its delectable food. In the evening, panjiri and panchamrit were prepared as prasad. We would decorate the temple and create a jhankhi (miniature display) using available toys. Baby Krishna would be placed in a cradle, and we would swing it back and forth.

Then came Ganesh Chaturthi, where Amma would fast, and besan ladoo would be offered as prasad. Laddoos seem to be a favorite of the gods. In the north, Lord Hanuman is also offered laddoos, mostly bundi laddoos. Outside temples in the north, there are often stalls selling laddoos on Tuesdays and Saturdays. In Maharashtra, Modak is offered as prasad to Lord Ganesh, and it is also round in shape. Hanuman is worshipped here as well, with devotees pouring oil and garlanding the idol on Saturdays.

In our colony, my Maharashtrian friend Kunda Chitale invited me to her house for Ganpati darshan, introducing me to the Maharashtrian style of celebrating Ganesh festival for the first time. Her door was adorned with beautiful rangoli designs, and I tasted modak for the first time. Later, I learned more about the Ganpati festival, including the decoration of pandals (temporary structures) and cultural programs held in various societies, followed by the grand visarjan (immersion) on the 10th day.

As Dussehra approached, Navratri would begin. Amma would observe a fast, and on the 9th day, nine girls would be invited for prasad. Puri, halwa, and small channa would be served, and each girl would receive a chawanni (25 paise coin) as dakshina. The girls were treated as manifestations of the goddess, and their feet would be washed first, followed by applying teeka (vermilion) on their foreheads, and then they would be fed. We would visit at least 3-4 houses in a group, and receiving the chawanni was a big attraction. Nowadays, in North India, this tradition is still celebrated, often called "Kanjak Puja," where under-privileged children are invited or money is given in temples.

Another surprise we learned through our colony friends was that Ram Leela (a dramatic reenactment of the Ramayana) used to be performed for 10 days in the ground behind our house. All the children would take mats (daris), have an early dinner, and secure a place to sit in front so that we could have a good view. It was a grand production with a large stage, depicting the entire epic of Ramayana in a professional manner, just like what we later watched on TV. The costumes were beautiful, the storytelling with songs and dialogues was captivating. We were engrossed in watching the performances, especially the fight scenes with bows and arrows. The 10th day would culminate in the final battle between Lord Ram and Ravana, where Ravana was defeated and burned, typically in a large ground in Bombay. It was a celebration of good triumphing over evil, and the memory of it remains etched in my mind.

In our house, on the day of Dussehra, mutton curry would be prepared, along with a sweet dish. In the evening, we children would go to different houses, offering apta leaves as a gesture of auspiciousness. This practice was called "Sona Patta."

Before Diwali, Sharad Purnima, also known as Kojagiri in Maharashtra, would be celebrated. Amma would observe a fast, and rice kheer (pudding) would be prepared as prasad. The kheer would be kept near a window where moonlight would fall throughout the night. It was believed that the moon's nectar would bless the kheer, making it taste delicious and chilled for breakfast the next morning.

Then came Karwa Chauth, an important fast observed by married women. Amma would observe the fast and prepare dishes like puri, pua (sweet puris), kadhi, chawal, and phara (salty gujia filled with chana dal, steamed). She would break her fast after sighting the moon and performing the puja.

Next was Diwali, our major festival spanning four days. First, on Dhanteras, Amma and Baboo would go and buy something new for the house. Then, on Narak Chaturdashi, we would apply ubtan (a herbal paste) and take an early morning bath. On Diwali, the house would be adorned with oil lamps and electric lights at the front door. Every year, we would buy new clay idols of Lord Laxmi and Lord Ganesh, and small kulhads (earthen cups) would be filled with lai batasha (sugar candy) and kept for puja along with other sweets. After the puja, bursting firecrackers would be a routine, followed by a festive dinner and playing the game of kaudi, using cowrie shells.

After Diwali, Bhai Dooj would be celebrated at home. We sisters would wake up early in the morning and draw various figures on the floor using yellow powder made from wet haldi (turmeric) and rice, such as the sun, moon, river, etc. Then we would perform the puja. Amma would narrate the story of Bhai Dooj, and we would symbolically kill the Yamdoot (the messenger of death) using a khalbatta (a grinding stone) by putting sindoor (vermilion) and betel nut on it, to protect our brothers from any harm. After that, we would apply teeka on our brothers' foreheads, tie a thread around their wrists, and they would give us some money as a token of love. We would be delighted and then allowed to eat something. We had to fast until we applied the teeka on our brothers.

Aumlata bua, Baboo's sister, used to send the teeka by post as per the custom, along with a letter specifying what she wanted as a gift. That was the best part, and Baboo always gave the gifts she asked for whenever we went to our hometown (gaon).

A day before Diwali, there would be a grand function at our railway club. Everyone would dress up and go to the club in the evening for a party, which included a spectacular fireworks show. Each child would receive a packet of firecrackers and a box of sweets. We would get Chandu Halwai's tin dabba filled with various colorful Karanchi halwa (a sweet dish). Six dabbas would come to our house, one for each child, and we would keep them separately to enjoy whenever we wanted. Baboo was working in Matunga at that time, and the Matunga club was bigger and a bit more upscale than the Parel club. New Year and Christmas parties were held in the Matunga club.

During Christmas, they would decorate a Christmas tree, have snacks, and there would be a party. Santa Claus would come and shake hands with the children, giving them chocolates. However, gifts were only given to those children whose parents paid for it, even though it was subsidized by the club. I received a badminton racket once, and my elder brother received a camera. The system wasn't appealing as some parents would give their children extravagant gifts, which made other children jealous. We only went to the Matunga club two or three times. The Parel club was better, as they provided the same type of sweet dabba to every child. There would be loud music and dance, and the big dance floor would be filled with many uncles, aunties, and my Christian friends dancing with their boyfriends.

So the year ended, and the new year arrived with Makar Sankranti. On this day, we would wake up early, take a bath, and Amma would have already made a heap of khichdi with til laddo, ghee, and salt for each one of us. We had to say "Krishna Krishna Arpane" and put a coin in it while touching and doing namaskar. After that, we were given til laddoo to eat. For lunch, we would have bajra sweet puri with til, called pua, and udad dal khichdi. The khichdi touched by us would be given to the temple in the evening along with some money. This tradition is still followed today.

In Maharashtra, Makar Sankranti is celebrated in a different way. People exchange til laddo or vadi with each other and say "Til gud ghya, godd godd bola" meaning have sweet sesame and jaggery and speak sweetly. Maharashtrian friends invite ladies for Haldi Kumkum, where everyone dresses up in traditional saris and jewellery. Haldi Kumkum is applied to the ladies' foreheads, and they are given small gifts as well.

My Punjabi school friends used to celebrate it as Lohri. They would bring rewadi and groundnuts to school the next day, and people would also fly kites on this day.

Then came Basant Panchami, on which day everyone would wear yellow dresses, and yellow Kesari chawal (saffron rice) would be made at home. Some Bengali friends of mine used to perform Saraswati Puja on this day. When we were young, yellow frocks would be stitched for us, and Amma would wear a yellow blouse or sari.

Then came Holi. One day before Holi, Holika Dahan would be celebrated. In our society, wood would be collected and lit in the evening. Ladies would perform puja by going around the bonfire. Some people would play drums and manjeera and sing lok geet. Prasad of gujia, a sweet dish, would be distributed. Amma had made a big dabba of Khoya Gujia and Besan Papari (thin gram flour papad) a few days ago, which we would eat for many days.

On the second day of Holi, a grand celebration would take place in the club. By 9 or 10 in the morning, everyone would come to the big hall and play Holi with dry colors. There would be cultural programs featuring local railway artists. Shailendra, a famous lyricist who worked with Raj Kapoor, would recite his poems and songs. Brunch would include samosas, kachoris, dahi vada, gulab jamun, and more. Mutton would also be prepared at home that day.

Baboo was an outgoing person, so we had many outings. We often went to the circus, as Baboo would get passes. I can still remember the tigers in cages, the ringmaster with a hunter making them perform tricks, girls doing aerobics and swinging tricks, jugglers with balls, and the joker who made us laugh.

We also watched many movies with our family and colony friends. We formed a group of 10 friends, and I still remember watching movies like Jagrati, Ham Panchi Ek Dal Ke, Boot Polish, The Ten Commandments, Ben-Hur, and more. As we grew up, the movie names changed, but our group remained intact. We even bought songbooks to learn the lyrics of the songs, which were sold during the movie interval.

Baboo had a wide circle of friends from different communities, including Bengalis, Muslims, Christians, Maharashtrians, and Hindi-speaking friends. We received Biryani during Bakri-id from Aziz Chacha and a big plum cake from a Christian friend whose name I can't remember, but I still recall the taste of the plum cake and I still love it. At that time, we used to call all of Baboo's friends "Chacha" and "Chachi" instead of uncle and aunty.

Close friends would visit each other and go for lunches or picnics. I remember 2 or 3 trips we went on, including visits to Lonavala and Matheran. We enjoyed the ride on the toy train, sang songs, and stayed there for one night. We also went to the Elephanta Caves by ferry with Gupta Chacha and Mathur Chacha's families, who were very close friends of Baboo.

Amma was orthodox and vegetarian. She would perform all the religious duties and fasts in our house but never insisted that we follow them. So we never used to fast, even though my friends who observed Sawan Somwar fast for a good husband told us about it. I did observe Monday fasts for many years, only eating at night.

During the summer, we would visit our native place, Ladgawa. Baboo would get three passes in a year, and we mostly used two of them to visit our native place twice. Afterward, due to higher studies, our visits to the village became less frequent. The third pass would be used for pilgrimages. We visited places like Mathura, Rameshwaram, Madurai, Allahabad, Benaras, Haridwar, and more.

I'll now share our visits to Ladgawa as a routine. Whatever I remember from my visits, I will narrate it as one visit.

Our journey to Ladgawa in Fatehpur, Uttar Pradesh, involved visiting Baboo's extended family. Baboo had three sisters and four brothers. He was the eldest, followed by Krishna Chacha, who was working in Kanpur, hence we called him "Kanpur wale Chacha." Then there were Hemlata Bua, Prem Lata, and Om Lata Bua. Om Lata was the youngest. Bishun Chacha had got married last year and was helping Baba with farming as he wasn't interested in studying. Laxmi Chacha was studying in Kanpur. Baba, Meva Lala Srivastava, was a prosperous landowner at that time, with many acres of land where rice, wheat, and sugarcane were cultivated. We also had orchards of mango, guava, and chiku. Baba had a commanding personality, tall and healthy, with a mustache. He looked quite impressive.

My Dadi, Girija Devi, was also an affectionate lady.

We started our journey to Fatehpur, catching a train from VT (now CST) station and reached Fatehpur, which was about 20 km away from our gaon. At the station, Laxmi Chacha was there with two ekkas to receive us. An ekka is like a tanga, but different in shape. The horses used for the ekkas were our own. Shyama Ghodi was Baba's favorite, and the other horse's name I can't remember now. We sat in both ekkas, and there would be a race between the two as we proceeded towards the gaon. Baboo's close cousin, Ramesh Chacha, would also accompany us sometimes, along with his sister, Pony Bua. Bua was of my age, and they used to stay in Fatehpur.

As we reached, Baba came out excitedly shouting, "See, Bahadur has come!" Bahadur was Baboo's pet name. Dadi and everyone came out, and Baba and Dadi hugged all of us affectionately. Customary charan sparsh was done by everyone. It was a very big house with a big terrace, angan, and a large chaupal or baramada on both sides of the entrance. In front, on the left, was a very big well from which water was supplied to some farms through a motor. Opposite the well was a big Hanuman temple where a pujari Pandit Chacha used to stay. His daughter would also play with us when we were there. Since Baboo was the eldest, I and Bade Bhaiya were also called Bade Bhaiya and Jiji by everyone. Kanpur Chacha also arrived with his family. By evening, it was a get-together of the family.

After settling down, we children went on an expedition to the mango garden as it was mango season. We wandered around in the mango groves until lunchtime, plucking and eating mangoes. We also enjoyed kamarakh fruit, which was sour in taste. We would sit, chat, and play for some time and then come back. We drank Panha and had a simple meal of arahar dal with raw mango, which made it very tasty. We also had some seasonal sabzi that was grown on a patch of land behind the temple, along with mango chili and garlic chutney or pickle, and cut onions. Chachi made garam roti on the chulha. We were so hungry that the food tasted really good.

In the evening, Baba would sit in the baramada or choupal, as it was called. Some villagers would come in the evening to chat with him, and we would be introduced to everyone as Bahadur's children who were studying in Bombay. Baba would proudly introduce us. The next day, we would sit in a bullock cart and visit some fields where farmers were plowing with bullocks. On one side, there would be a big wheel-like machine going round, which was used for cutting crops.

At our ancestral house in Fatehpur with my grand-parents (sitting on the ground-second row- fourth from left)

In the evening, everyone would sit in the angan, and small mangoes would be kept in water in a bucket. We would sit around and enjoy sucking on mangoes one after another. Big Kalami aam were also of very good quality grown there. They were kept in bhusa for ripening. At night, after dinner, Dadi would tell engrossing stories of raja, rani, and thugs. In the evening, there used to be an aarti at the Hanuman temple with a ghanta and manjeera.

During winter, the scene was different with a guava garden instead of mangoes, and fields all around with sugarcane. There was a man who would cut the sugarcane and give it to us to chew. Gur (jaggery) was also made, so we saw how gur was made. Sugarcane juice was taken out from the kolhu (bullocks going round the sugarcane put in a machine) and put in a big karahi for thickening. When it was about to be made, some of it was taken out, which was called raab and kept aside to eat as it is. The rest was made into big round bhelies of gur. Raab was very tasty to eat with ghee roti. Vinegar was also made from sugarcane juice. The juice was kept in big jars of chini mitti and covered and kept in a dark small room. Dadi used to tell us that after 3 months, it becomes vinegar.

One sweet dish called rasewar was also made with rice and sugarcane juice. Rice was boiled with sugarcane juice in a big batua, a round pot, on a slow fire. Some dry fruits fried in ghee were put in it and cooked on a slow fire for a long time. It used to be very tasty.

In the morning, we children, along with Dadi, used to go and pick channa or sarson ka saag or harbara, whatever was in season, or peas and small tomatoes, and bring them home. We would clean the saag with

Dadi, and then it was cooked in a batua. Sometimes, it was eaten with bajra roti. In winter, bajra roti was eaten with gur and ghee too.

In the evening, everyone would sit around the fire and chat. All the brothers, Baboo, Baba, and we elder children would be on one side. They used to laugh loudly, cracking jokes, and the loudest voice was of Bishun Chacha. When they were all together, they were very jovial. We would also sit for some time and then go to sleep. This picture is from one of my trips when I was young.

On the return journey from gaon, gud, mangoes, dal, bari, etc., whatever the season, were kept in one big tin box to carry with us to Bombay. Wheat and rice were booked in the break van of the same train so that it could also reach with us. In those days, there was rationing, so we would get a limited supply of grains from the ration shop. Outside in the open market, things were costly and not of good quality, so bringing grains from gaon used to be helpful. As guests were also a permanent feature, we would come back and get back to our routine. But next year, Bua's marriage was fixed, and the preparations started at home. At that time, a tailor used to be called to stitch dresses for all of us whenever required. Colorful frocks with zari borders and pink garara kurta were stitched. Garara was like sharara, and nowadays, a dupatta with zari gota was added. Blouses were also designed and stitched for Amma. The preparations for gifts for Bua had started as we received a list from the gaon.

The marriage of my bua holds some vivid memories in my mind. The baratis stayed in big tents under mango trees. There was a week-long feast of food, ladies dancing, and gaana with dholak. We also danced to songs in our pink garara, kurta, and chunni. The big petromax lamps and kerosene lamps gave a beautiful view at night, almost like a movie. The next day, bua sat in a decorated palki while going from the house to the bus where the baratis had arrived. That's what I remember.

One more thing I just remembered: Once, we had gone to Ramesh Chacha's house in Fatehpur. We all went to watch a comedy movie in a small theater. It was interesting to see that all the gents were sitting downstairs, while the balcony was reserved for ladies. Even though Chacha and the others were laughing loudly downstairs, we could hear them from upstairs. It was a good change.

Afterwards, we went for mama's marriage too. We traveled to Jhansi and met a different set of relatives. The atmosphere there was musical. Every evening, after dinner, everyone would gather and sing. One of my cousins played the flute so well, I still remember. That's why Amma must have been gifted with a harmonium during her marriage, although she never got a chance to play it due to her household activities. I also learned to play the harmonium for some time, playing bhajans and other songs. The harmonium given to me is still with me as a memento of Amma. Bade Bhaiya also used to sing and play the harmonium during those days. His favorite song was "Baba Man Ki Ankhe Khol" and songs by Saigal. He sang well during his school days.

Time passed gradually, and there I was in the 11th standard, studying in the year 1958-59. There was no special treatment for SSC exams at home like nowadays. As I was interested, I used to study whenever I had the time, without much pressure. That year, my subjects were Hindi, English, Gujarati, General Science (Physics, Chemistry, and Biology), Elementary Maths (Algebra, Geometry, and Arithmetic), and Social Studies (History, Geography, and Civics). It was the last year of school, and I knew I was going to miss school life. We friends would be separated and miss each other, the interval gossip, the excitement and thrill of inter-school kho-kho and langadi matches, sack races, obstacle races, three-legged races, and relay races. I won many prizes for running, and I kept four cups and one medal in the drawing room showcase. After the half-yearly exams, we friends went for a movie and had fun before bidding goodbye to our school days and heading to different colleges.

Then there was a group photo of our class and a party organized by the school. I have enjoyed reminiscing about my school life while writing this. I just remembered a poem by Subhadra Kumari Chauhan:

"Bar Bar Aati Hai Mujhko Madhur Yaad Bachpan Teri, Gaya Lai Gaya Tu Jeevan Ki Sabse Mast Khushi Meri" (I keep remembering the sweet memories of my childhood again and again; you took them away, what brought the greatest joy to my life).

Finally, our final exams were over, and the vacation began.

With my friends (seated in the center)

Finally, my SSC (Secondary School Certificate) result came. I missed getting first class by 2 marks, but everyone, including me, was happy. I got admission to Ram Narain Ruia College in Arts, which was one of the reputed colleges near Matunga at that time.

It was the first day of college in July 1959. Dressed in a loose salwar kurta, I entered the college campus, feeling excited and nervous. The college was huge, with multiple entrances and floors. Students were running here and there, and finally, I located my class on the 2nd floor, F.Y. Sec B. There were about 150 students, mostly girls. There was one group of South Indian girls clad in half sarees, and they were confidently answering all the questions asked by the professors on the first day since they were fluent in English. The college was an English medium institution, and most students came from different medium schools like Hindi, Marathi, and Gujarati. However, within a few days, the situation changed.

My college timings were from 8 am to 2 pm, as it was a morning college. My subjects for the intermediate level were Hindi, English, Sanskrit, History, and Economics. For Hindi and Sanskrit, we had to go to different classes. In the Hindi class, I made friends within a week. We were a group of 7 girls, and Premlata and Kokila became my close friends throughout our intermediate years. To improve my English, apart from the course books, I started reading English magazines like Femina from our railway library, and it was during this time that my love for Mills and Boon novels began. The college also had a very good library.

On the home front, things had also changed. We had a new addition to our home, a Murphy radio on which morning bhajans and instrumental music were played. At that time, my siblings and I were interested in listening to "Binaca Geetmala," a popular music radio show that aired from 8 to 9 on Wednesdays. Amma had also joined the railway ladies club and showcased her cooking skills in various cooking competitions held there. I attended a Bengali sweets course at the club, where I learned to make rasgulla, chamcham, raskadam, hing kachori, and launglatika. I still remember those recipes. Whatever I learned in class, I would try to make at home as well.

In college, my studies went along with extracurricular activities and spending time with friends watching movies. Instead of ragada pattice that we ate in school, we started eating masala dosa, which used to cost 20 paise.

I developed an interest in the Hindi section of the college magazine. Inspired by poetess Mahadevi Varma, I wrote a poem for the magazine and even won the second prize for it.

All the professors were very good, but I can't forget the English professor. He used to roam around the classroom and explain everything in very simple English. "Silas Marner," a novel by George Eliot, was in our syllabus, and I still remember the novel after so many years because of how well he taught it.

In Sanskrit, we studied Kalidas. His plays, "Meghadoot" and "Shakuntala," gave us a basic knowledge of Sanskrit.

Meanwhile, there were two important shows that Babu took us to in those days. The first one was "Holiday on Ice." It was a big skating rink with a platform made of ice, where artists performed dances while skating in different styles. They went round the whole platform, and the searchlights from above created a beautiful effect. It was a memorable show. Thinking back I am amazed that such shows were held in Mumbai and that I had the good fortune of seeing it.

Another memorable show was "Circarama." It was a dome-like theater with a big platform inside, surrounded by 11 fixed cameras and perfectly synchronized projectors. We stood in the center as a circular film presentation took us on a cruise to different places, from the East to the West Coast. It was a wonderful experience and I am really grateful to Baboo for giving us such exposures at such a young age.

My family (seated second from left)

Meanwhile, Baboo had decided to settle in Lucknow and purchased a plot of land. So, our visits to Lucknow started every year. Let me introduce you to Amma's cousin, Shanta Mausi, who lived in Lucknow at that time. Keshav Mausa and Shanta Mausi had four children: Madhuri, who was older than Bade Bhaiya; Meera, who was my age; Rajeev, who was Harish's age; and Anil, providing company for all of us. The plot was purchased near their house in Ameenabad, the heart of the city. We have very good memories of our visits during those times. Meera and Madhuri were both adventurous and loved exploring the city, eating chat, kulfi, kachori, watching many movies, and going on picnics. The Shaheed Smarak, which was opened at that time, had boating facilities and was a hot spot. In winter, we enjoyed gajak and rewadi. Nothing can beat Lucknow when it comes to food. The whole family was talkative. Mausaji was a skilled sitar player, and there were often classical music gatherings in their house, with people sitting on masanads and gaddas. Otherwise, we children would sing songs, chat, and enjoy on the terrace after dinner. It was a lot of fun.

Back in Bombay, you had to have some filmy connections. Bhagwan-dada, a famous comedian of those days, had a brother-in-law who worked under Baboo. So, whenever there were shooting passes available, we would go. His studio was near Raj Kapoor's studio in Chembur. Once, I went to a shooting and saw a fight scene and a dance scene. There were so many repetitions, and it was quite boring to watch. Bhagwan's film "Albela" with Geeta Bali was a hit at that time. His wife had organized a special show for it, and Amma attended the haldi kumkum ceremony at Hindmata Talkies. I went along with Amma, and the hall was filled with ladies who were given gazra, haldi kumkum, and pedha at the entrance. It was a nice movie, and I still enjoy its songs and dances.

I passed my intermediate exams in 1961 and decided to specialize in philosophy, pursuing a B.A. Honors degree. All eight papers were in philosophy, including two papers on psychology (Indian and Western) and political philosophy. I learned about many philosophers such as Dr. Radhakrishnan, an Indian philosopher, and Western philosophers like Aristotle and Plato.

My close friend at that time was Vinod, our immediate neighbor. So, this year I attended the college day event with her. It used to be held in the late evening and had a very big gathering. Everyone was dressed up, and after the cultural program, there was a segment where fishponds were distributed. It was the most interesting part. Titles were given to students and even some professors. Ajit Wadekar, who later became a famous cricketer, was our senior, and his girlfriend was in the first year. Both of them were called on stage, and titles were given to them, followed by applause from everyone. It was a light-hearted moment enjoyed by all.

Meanwhile, Baboo got transferred to VT, where he was in charge of the air-conditioned bogie. At that time, there was only one air-conditioned bogie. So, whenever any VIPs traveled, Baboo accompanied them. Dr. Rajendra Prasad, the President, often traveled with the family by train. On one occasion, Mrs. Jacqueline Kennedy also traveled by train with her sister, and Baboo had the opportunity to take a picture with them. Mrs. Jacqueline was as charming and famous at that time as Diana is now.

My father (extreme right) with Dr. Rajendra Prasad

My father (extreme right) receiving Pandit Nehru

In the meantime, in Amma's ladies club, there was a one-year stitching diploma course using Usha sewing machines. Amma enrolled me in that course. While learning stitching, I stitched dresses for all family members, including frocks, blouses, salwars, kurtas, and even shirts for Harish. But it didn't end there. After that, I joined a machine embroidery course taught by a Sindhi lady. I made many tablecloths while learning different stitches. The hand machine was converted into a leg machine by adding pedals to it.

Apart from my studies, my love for reading novels continued.

In 1962, during the India-China war, Mr. Nehru appealed to everyone, especially ladies, to donate gold. A big procession of famous actors of that time passed through the city in trucks to collect funds. The hit pair from the movie "Junglee," Shammi Kapoor and Saira Banu, were the main attraction. Shammi Kapoor was singing the song "Mere Yaar Shabba Khair." We also went to see the procession with friends. Some girls even gave their earrings and rings, as they were infatuated with Shammi Kapoor. At home, they must have received a scolding for it.

Finally, my B.A. final exams were in March 1963. Before that, Baboo got promoted and transferred to Jabalpur. After our exams, we were shifting to Jabalpur. Some of my relatives, who had not visited Bombay so far, came to visit us when they heard the news of Baboo's transfer. So, we had to say goodbye to the city of dreams. There were many farewell parties as we had stayed there for so long. Goodbye, Bombay, but once you've lived in Bombay, you can't forget it. That's the magic of the city. Some of Baboo's friends had already decided to settle there.

PART 3

A New Life Begins With Marriage - 1962 To 1965 at Jabalpur

So, finally, we landed in Jabalpur during the scorching summer heat of Madhya Pradesh, which was a stark contrast to Bombay. The house in Jabalpur was a grand bungalow from the British era, with a spacious drawing room, dining area, and bedrooms. The ceilings were high, and there were long hanging rods for ceiling fans. Each room had a fireplace for heating during the extreme winters since the climate there was quite variable. In front of the bungalow, there was a well-maintained lawn and a small road leading to a large opening gate. Beautiful roses were planted on both sides of the road, adding to the charm. We were filled with joy.

Behind the bungalow, there were six servant quarters at some distance, meant for the washerman, gardener, cleaner, and others. It was a great perk for government servants at that time. The location of the house was also excellent, situated in Civil Lines. There were two nearby cinemas, Liberty Talkies and Empire Talkies, with Empire Talkies being owned by Premnath, a famous actor of that era (his latest film was "Bobby"). There was also the Railway Club, which had facilities like table tennis, a wooden badminton court, and a library. What more could one ask for?

After settling down, I got admitted to the College of Social Psychology & Guidance, which was affiliated with P.S.M. (Psychological Society of Madhya Pradesh) for pursuing a Master's degree in Applied Social Psychology. It was a relatively new subject at that time, with courses focused on social psychology, child development, psychoanalysis, and applied psychology. The main purpose was to learn how to solve social problems related to the mind.

It was a two-year course, and in the final year, we had to write a thesis. I chose child development as the topic for my thesis. The college had timings from 10 am to 4 pm and had a well-equipped library with reference books and journals. Among my close group of friends were Anjali Jha, Pratima Nagarkar, Jyotsna Naik, Navaz Garda (a Parsi friend), and Lini Thakurdas (a Christian friend who stayed in the hostel). Lini became a frequent visitor to my house and one of my best friends. Her father was a pastor in charge of a church in Indore, and through her, I learned many new things about Christianity and how they are always supportive of each other.

After learning about Plato and Aristotle during my B.A., it was now time to explore the works of Alfred Freud, the psychologist. Our professors were all knowledgeable, and Mr. Gurnani, who taught social psychology, was particularly kind and helpful. Another professor, Ms. Sethna, was in charge of my thesis. She was a Parsi lady who always dressed in a traditional Parsi style, with her sari's pallu in the front and her hair styled in the Parsi manner. She was young, bright, and an excellent professor.

On the home front, the club in Jabalpur was very socially active, especially the ladies' club as it was run by some Maharashtrian ladies. There were numerous cultural activities organized by the club. After a few weeks, the club organized a picnic to Bhedaghat, which was attended by about 25 families. Cooks accompanied us, and we had food cooked on-site along with some games to play. Bhedaghat was famous for its waterfall known as Dhuandhar Ghat. It was a breathtaking sight where the Narmada River flowed through milky white marble rocks, creating a natural waterfall. Boating was also available, making it a delightful trip. We also visited Bhedaghat on a full moon night during Kojagiri (Sharad Purnima), and the experience of boating under the moonlight was truly magical. We enjoyed a delicious dinner of puri bhaji and basundi (or rabadi). There was a temple in

Bhedaghat where one could find marble showpieces of various gods' statues and other items like agarbatti stands. Hursa, a tool used for making chapattis, was particularly famous there. The movie "Jis Desh Mein Ganga Behti Hai" directed by Raj Kapoor was also shot there. One of the ghats was later named Mandakini.

We also visited another ghat called Gauri Ghat with a small group of Baboo's friends. The cook prepared vati (a type of bread) and baingan (eggplant) bharta over an open fire. The taste of bharata and vati with generous amounts of ghee still makes my mouth water when I think about it.

In Jabalpur, my mother (Amma) became actively involved in the club's activities. On the 15th of August and 26th of January, after flag hoisting, all the ladies, including my mother, dressed impeccably in white saris, would go to the RLW Hospital to distribute fruits to the patients. One Mrs. Sanyal used to teach sitar at the club, and my inclination to learn awakened. I immediately joined her class and learned the basics of sitar for a year before getting married.

Apart from our regular studies, we had guest lecturers coming to the college every Friday. One such guest lecturer was Acharya Rajneesh, who came dressed in a pure white silk robe. There was something captivating about his speech, and we were all mesmerized by it. Few years later, he gained worldwide fame, as we all know now. Although we couldn't fully comprehend his philosophy at that time, we now admire him for it.

Meanwhile, the search for a suitable boy for me was in full swing. One Swami Sevanand Ji, who was originally a Kayastha and had become a Swami, dressed in an orange robe, used to visit us, as well as many other Kayastha families, to do match-making. He hailed from Jhansi, and since both my mother and mother-in-law were from Jhansi, there was a common connection that helped move the marriage proposal forward. Match-making was his part-time job.

He brought the proposal of my future husband, who was in the final year of engineering at Raipur, to my parents. Among the other proposals that were there, he was shortlisted by my parents, and I was selected by the boy's parents. Horoscopes were matched by pandits, and everything seemed to be in order, so the alliance proceeded.

Their visits became more frequent, and they would come and chat with me for some time as well. My father-in-law was a lawyer at Jabalpur High Court. Things were being finalized, but my father-in-law did not inform his son about the marriage, as it may disturb his studies according to him. So the engagement, or "bariksha" as it was called, was fixed on Basant Panchami in the first week of February.

On the day of the engagement, about 20 relatives came for lunch, including one of my husband's classmates, Prabhakar Naik. As soon as the ceremony was over, he went home and informed my husband that our marriage was fixed. As soon as my husband got to know, he came to see me by somehow visiting my college without my knowledge.

After the engagement, my in-laws started visiting us more frequently in the evening. Whenever they would come, the tea set were taken out, serve hot snacks like pakori, and they would discuss marriage. My siblings were happy as they used to bring rabadi in kulhad, whenever they came. Sometimes, my in-laws would pick me up in the car if they wanted me to meet some of their relatives. They even took me for saree shopping once, though the saree was selected by them. Finally, the date of the marriage was fixed for May 13th. Meanwhile, my first-year exams also got over, and preparations for the marriage started in full swing.

A trip to Benaras was planned to purchase sarees for the marriage, for me and other relatives from both sides. So we went to Benaras. My mother, father, and I went shopping. As we had first-class passes, traveling was not a problem. We visited some interior shops in the narrow lanes of Benaras. For me, a Dhani-colored zari silk Benarasi saree was chosen as the main saree, along with two more heavy Benarasi silk sarees. After purchasing sarees for many relatives as well, we enjoyed delicious kachori sabji and lassi in one of the gallis of Benaras. The lassi was awesome. The next day, we took a dip in the river Ganga before returning.

Four days before the marriage, another ceremony called the Tilak ceremony was held. My eldest brother, Baboo, and my siblings went to my in-laws' place with a big plate of rice, seven supari (betel nut), haldi pieces, a sweet token, and some suit pieces and sarees for the boy and his family. This ceremony finalized the marriage. Here, my husband became friends with my eldest brother, and the next day, he came to our house in his car. Since he couldn't take me out alone, he took all of us to Kenburry Coffee House in Sadar.

Now comes the actual marriage on May 13th, 1964. It was the first marriage in the family, and my maternal grandmother was there, as usual. Keshav Mausa and Shanta Mausi, who were very close to us, came from Lucknow. Madhuri Jia had already gotten married, and Meera was studying medicine, so only Rajeev came with them. Mausa Ji was in charge of catering, so we called halwais (sweet makers) who made a variety of sweets, including laddoos, mathari, khurma (both sweet and salty), and balushai. Big matharis called suhal and big bundi laddoos were also made, which were supposed to be sent to the groom's house in a big tokni (basket) and given to all the relatives when they left after the marriage. All the sweets were stored in one room, and Mausa Ji was in charge of it. Rajeev must have been helping him throughout, as he later became a well-known caterer in Lucknow.

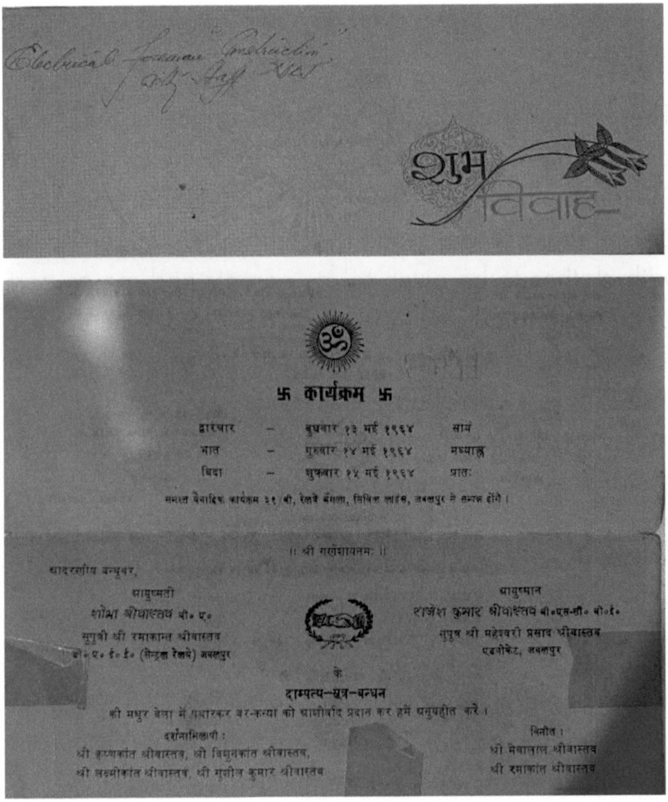

My Wedding Card

More relatives gradually arrived at our place, including my father and paternal grandmother from the village. Baba had become paralyzed a few days back, so a servant accompanied him to take care of him. Our immediate neighbour, Mr. Ghosh, had given half of his bungalow for our relatives to stay. The next day was the Mandap ceremony. The mandap was set up and decorated, and a pandit came to perform some puja, inviting all the ancestors for the marriage through mantras.

The following day was the haldi ceremony, where a paste of turmeric and oil is applied to the bride by all the girls and ladies. Thakur Prasad Nana (maternal uncle), Rajjan Mama, and Mami from Jhansi were there with clothes to be given to my parents and me as part of the custom. The day after that, the "chuddi" ceremony took place, where a bundle of bangles was brought. In those days, glass bangles were a must, and all the ladies would wear at least a dozen bangles on one hand. They would come and choose bangles under the mandap of their choice. Then, the "naunn" would come with a container of alta (red liquid color) and apply it to all the ladies' feet. Alta is usually applied on all festive occasions.

From that day onwards, Shanta Mausi, who was in charge of the dholak (traditional drum), would sit, and a mehfil (gathering) of dance and song would start. She was very fond of singing and dancing. The songs sung at the girl's place are called "bannee," while at the boy's place, they are called "banna." It was a very interesting and enjoyable time. There was no fixed day like the ladies' Sangeet, so the music would go on daily until the time of the marriage.

The atmosphere at home was filled with joy, but Baboo and Amma seemed tense and anxious, hoping that everything would go smoothly. The ladies, on the other hand, were mostly relaxed and joyous. They enjoyed eating, dressing up in their finery, gossiping, and taking advantage of the opportunity to meet after a long time.

Finally, on the evening of May 13th, the baraat (the groom's wedding procession) arrived with a band and music. Although it was a local marriage, they arrived very late because the relatives took a long time to get ready, causing everyone to wait. The first ceremony was the dwarchar, where the groom's puja (worship) was performed by the pandit (priest), with Baboo and Bade Bhaiya participating. After that, all the baratis (members of the groom's procession) were welcomed and garlanded. This was followed by the milani ceremony, where the relatives from both sides were introduced to each other. Snacks and sherbet were served, and then the jaimala ceremony took place.

After that, a lavish dinner followed, accompanied by ice cream. It also served as a reception for Baboo's colleagues and Amma's ladies club friends. My college friends were also present, as were many of my husband's friends from Raipur. The gathering consisted of a large crowd of young friends and relatives from both sides, who enjoyed themselves the most. Finally, the events of the first day concluded after dinner, and the caterer began preparations for the second day.

After dinner, the actual marriage ceremony began around midnight. Most of the elderly people went to sleep after dinner, and only those who were required for the rituals stayed to play their parts. Friends and young relatives attended to enjoy the festivities. I wore a yellow saree, as per custom, while my husband came dressed in a jamaa, a cloak-type dress, and a pagadi (turban) on his head. I also wore a small mor (peacock feather) on my head and had a gunghat (veil). The rituals commenced with kanyadaan, where parents give their daughter to the husband. It's a strange custom, but still followed, as the girl whom parents have brought up with so much love and affection is handed over to an unknown person.

After that, all the relatives, including chachas, chachis, mamis, and nanis, came forward to touch the girl's feet and give her gifts. The brother of the bride played an important role in the lava parsai ritual. Numerous other rituals followed for about two hours, and then the pheras (circumambulation) around the sacred fire took place. The youngsters enjoyed themselves, chatting and joking, while we followed the instructions of the pandit. I don't remember the specific vachans (sacred verses) recited by the pandit at that time. Finally, the marriage concluded around 4 o'clock.

The next day, a lunch called bhaat was organized, where only kachha khana (simple food) such as kadhi pakodi, dahi bade, dal, rice, roti, kesar bhat (sweet rice), or phirni were served, along with other eatables. The lunch was sponsored by the girl's mama (maternal uncle), so he had to contribute to it. Lunch was eaten under the mandap (decorated canopy) while sitting on the floor and using pattals (leaf plates) served by relatives.

In the evening, the kalewa ceremony took place. The groom, along with his younger siblings and friends, arrived dressed up, and gifts were given to the groom. Baboo gifted a Japanese transistor, which was quite new at that time (although it later became difficult to find batteries for it), and Amma gave a ring. Other relatives also gave gifts. Boys who accompanied the groom were given money in handkerchiefs by Amma. The kalewa ceremony concluded in the evening, followed by dinner once again.

The next morning, on the 15th, the bidai (departure) took place. In the morning, under the mandap, some rituals were performed. I felt a sense of sadness and apprehension about leaving my home and entering my sasural (in-laws' home). It was a challenging time for everyone, especially the parents. Amma, Nani, and Mausi could express their emotions and cry, but Baboo though very sad was trying to control himself in every way. Ultimately, the girl had to leave her home. I carried a large tin box filled with my clothes and bags containing my accessories. I accompanied my husband in a black Ford car and arrived at my in-laws' place, which was located in Right Town.

Me and my husband – the newly weds

As I entered the new house and embarked on a new phase of life, my mother-in-law welcomed me with an aarti. In those days, ladies didn't go to the baraat (wedding procession). They would stay at home, singing and waiting for the baraat to return, creating much excitement and enthusiasm among them to see the bride. Now, I became the center of attention for everyone. Thanks to Hindi movies, everyone was familiar with the wedding rituals. After some time, I changed into another saree and showed my face to the relatives. I received a gold set as a gift from my mother-in-law and other relatives gifted me according to their relationship with the family. Gold was inexpensive back then, and relatives mostly gave gold rings or earrings as gifts.

After a break for lunch, there was some time to relax. In the evening, we had tea and engaged in gossip, followed by a late dinner. After that, I was asked to press my mother-in-law's feet. It was late by the time I finally got a chance to go to my room, where my husband was eagerly waiting. After some introduction and chatting, he gifted me a blue studded ring. Since I was told to wake up early the next morning, we eventually went to sleep after some formalities.

Before I continue, let me introduce you to my husband's family:

- My husband's name is Rajesh Srivastava, but he is more commonly known by his nickname Munnan. He also had another nickname, Tuntun, given to him by my father-in-law.
- My father-in-law's name is Maheshwari Prasad Srivastava, and he was an advocate in the Jabalpur High Court. We used to call him Chacha. My mother-in-law's name is Laxmi, and we used to call her Chachi.

My father-in-law had an elder brother named Vindeshwari Prasad, whom we referred to as Baboo. He was also an advocate in Satna. His wife was known as Badi Chachi, and she was his second wife (after the untimely demise of his first wife).

They had nine children, two from his first wife- Gomati & Virendra and seven children from his second wife:

Suresh, Awedesh, Asha, Bachha, Baby, Shashi, and Pappu.

Gomati Jijji, was married to Mr. Govindaprasad Srivastava.. Jijji had six children: Munni, Chunni, Guddi, Achhu, Bhaiya, and Pinki.

Virendra, whom everyone called Lallan Bhaiya, was a lecturer in Rewa. His wife was Shakun, and they had two daughters Anju and Ranju and a son Piyush.

My mother-in-law, Chachi, had five miscarriages before my husband was born. Due to the joint family system, Jijji (Gomati) and Lallan Bhaiya (Virendra) used to stay with Chacha and Chachi, the probable reason they were referred to as Chacha and Chachi by everyone, including my husband.

Although I received a warm welcome, I was told to wake up early, take a bath, and be ready before everyone else. With the help of a handheld mirror, I put on a bindi and sindoor, which were mandatory. I adorned myself with some ornaments, including heavy payal (anklets) on my feet, and then went out to touch the feet of all the elders. The next day, I was introduced to the kitchen by making gulgula (sweet pakoras). Shakun bhabhi (sister-in-law) was a great help during this time.

On the following day, the Kirtan Mandali (a group of women who perform devotional songs) was called for mu dikhai. They sang bhajans accompanied by the dholak and manjeera for about two hours, followed by snacks. Every Tuesday, there used to be a kirtan at someone's house.

After three days, Bade Bhaiya (elder brother-in-law) came to take me for the pagphera ceremony. I went home and returned after three days when my husband came to take me back, as was the custom. By this time, most of the rituals were over, and some relatives started to leave. While leaving, the ladies were gifted saris, and husbands and children were given money and sweets. Only his uncles' family and a few close relatives remained.

Now I had the opportunity to observe my surroundings. My mother-in-law, whom I now called Chachi, was slightly heavy with big glasses. She wore starched cotton sarees, her hair properly oiled and combed into a plait, and a big bindi on her forehead. Most of the time, she would sit on a low wooden stool called a modha, which was like a knitted cot. My father-in-law, Chacha, was a strict disciplinarian and very punctual in everything, from morning routines to dinner and even eating paan (betel leaf). Everyone seemed to be scared of him. Although I had met him before at our house, I had a different perception of him at that time.

I also remember Chachi's pet parrot, Mitthu. There was a cage hanging near the back door with the parrot inside. Everyone used to call him Mitthu, and he would utter words like "Ram Ram" and "Chachi." There was a bowl of water, green chilies, and a piece of fruit in his cage. As people entered the house, they would greet him with "Ram Ram," and he would respond. After taking a bath in the morning, Chachi would spend an entire hour at the temple where three Laddo Gopals, brass deities, were placed. They would be bathed daily, dressed up like children, and then worshipped with puja and aarti. In winter, they would be covered with a blanket at night, and during the month of Sawan, they would be placed on a swing (jhula). Both Chacha and Chachi were very orthodox and followed rituals strictly. Both my father-in-law and husband would recite the Hanuman Chalisa after their bath. It was all new to me. Additionally, whenever we traveled anywhere, all the Laddo Gopals would also accompany us in a cane basket, even on trains.

Lunch was served on a phul thali (platter) and offered to the gods before anyone could eat. In the evening, before dinner, aarti would be performed in front of a small Krishna temple with the ringing of bells, ghanta (metal bell), and manjeera (hand cymbals).

Food habits were also different. For breakfast, they mostly had tikiya (a salty snack) every day. The food was generally more oily, and they preferred spicy food. The men would always eat first, followed by the ladies. While the entire day was fine, dinner would be served very late, around 9 PM, as my father-in-law was a slow eater. The whole dinner routine would take about an hour. After dinner, around 10 PM, we would get a chance to go to sleep after cleaning the kitchen and completing other chores. Gradually, I got used to this routine.

For making lunch, a cook called Maharaj-ji used to come. The food was cooked on a chulha (traditional stove). I would observe him as I had to learn cooking later on. Lal bhaji (red spinach) was a compulsory dish for lunch, and green chutney had to be freshly ground every day on a silbatta (stone grinder). Traditional thalis (plates) were served, with a fixed place for each food item—first salt, then chutney, salad, sabzi (vegetable dish), daal (lentils), rice, and roti. Nothing could be placed out of order. After lunch, paan (betel leaf) was eaten. There was a paandaan (box for betel leaves) for making paan, a large sarota (knife) for cutting supari (betel nut), and a metal paandaan with wet chuna (lime powder) and kattha (catechu) in separate compartments. Paan leaves were kept in a wet cloth. I also gradually learned how to use the sarota, even though I cut my hands many times. Another thing I learned gradually was using the khalbatta (stone mortar and pestle) and silbatta.

All my Satna cousins stayed until the end of the month. Asha, who was of my age, became very friendly, and Shakun bhabhi (sister-in-law) was also affectionate, teaching me new things about my sasural (in-laws' home) as the senior daughter-in-law. The whole day would pass in eating and chatting. Afternoon siestas were common for all the ladies, with a hand fan in hand, as there was only one table fan in the room, which was not sufficient.

During that time, movies were the only form of entertainment. My husband and his cousins would often go to the movies. One day, as usual, they went for a movie after lunch but came back after some time because the theaters were closed due to the demise of Pandit Nehru, our first Prime Minister. It was shocking news for the nation, and like everyone else, I admired Chacha Nehru (as he was called) at that time. His birthday used to be celebrated as Children's Day. I had also read his book "Letters to Daughter Priyadarshini," which were letters addressed to Indira Gandhi from prison. They were very well written. He was very popular during those days, and over 1.5 million people from across the country attended his funeral.

After a few days, Vat Amavasya, the first festival after marriage, arrived. On this day, wives fast for the long life of their husbands. Being the first time, I had to dress up properly in a heavy sari and jewellery, especially a big round nose ring, which was compulsory for all festivals, and alta (red dye) on the feet. We went by car to a nearby big banyan tree. It was a very colorful sight there, with many ladies dressed in colorful saris performing puja and tying threads around the banyan tree. There is a legend of Savitri and Satyavan where Savitri saved the life of her husband by performing puja, so all ladies follow the same tradition. Each lady carried a lota (water vessel), puja thali (plate) with seasonal fruits and sweets, small round balls made of wheat flour, ghee, and jaggery, a baans (bamboo) hand fan. It was very interesting to watch some ladies fanning the tree and pressing their feet against the tree trunk after tying the thread. It was fascinating to see the rituals people followed. We also tied a thread around the tree, performed a simple puja, and returned.

After a few days, my husband got a job at Universal Cables Ltd. in Satna. Other relatives gradually left, and he joined his first job in Satna. My college also started after a few days, and I had to complete my M.A. final exams. So, parallelly, my college life and married life started. Since it was the first year of my marriage, we had to celebrate all the festivals, and I would frequently visit my parents' house for those occasions, where Chacha and Chachi were also invited. However, I would always stay back for a few days. My husband would come on some weekends, and sometimes we would go out to the coffee house, his favorite place, but we would not be completely truthful at home, saying that we were going to visit relatives. Chacha was very strict and against going to hotels or movies, so my husband would either lie at home or tell Chachi. There was a significant generation gap between father and son.

Whenever I was at my parents' house, I would go alone to college. But after marriage, Chacha would take me in his car if he had a case that day, as the high court was near our college. At other times, we would use a cycle rickshaw for traveling during those times.

The Jabalpur High Court was very huge, old, and an impressive British-era building. My friend Jyotsna Naik's father was a justice in the high court. Sometimes, while coming back from college, I would accompany her. Once, she took me inside her father's chamber as she had some work with him. I saw a courtroom for the first time, even though I had seen them in movies before.

In college, I mostly studied in the library as I had to write my thesis that year. I visited different schools to collect data for my thesis. I think I wrote my thesis on "Child Development Connected to Different Forms of Expression," but I can't remember exactly. I had my thesis printed and bound in my favorite blue color, as far as I can recall. I don't know what happened to it afterward. The year passed like this, and my final exams for M.A. were over. That marked the end of my college life, which never comes back. I bid farewell to my college friends and the college itself with a heavy heart.

With College Friends (standing first on the left)

After a few days, my husband came to take all of us to Satna, where he had rented a house. It was the first time I felt like I was going to my sasural. Although my parents' house was local, I used to spend half of my time there. They would also visit us frequently. Going to college, I didn't feel anything because I was so busy enjoying the new changes in my life. By that time, I was already pregnant with my first child. So, with a heavy heart, I said goodbye to Jabalpur and shifted to Satna.

PART 4

Motherhood Brings New Learnings - 1965 To 1968 at Satna

So here we were in Satna, a small place in Madhya Pradesh, settling into our comfortable rented house with an aangan (courtyard), kitchen, and two bedrooms. The weather was scorching hot as it was summer. My husband would ride his bicycle to his job at Universal Cables Ltd., which was about 20 kilometers away. We started visiting his uncle, who was a lawyer and lived in Satna city, and they would also come to our place. These visits became a routine.

After some time, we decided to visit Rewa, my husband's birthplace, where they used to live before shifting to Jabalpur. We went to their old house and visited some temples as well. Another frequent visitor was Mr. J.S. Varma, an advocate and our maternal uncle, who was a famous practicing lawyer at that time.

He used to stay near our house but later shifted to Jabalpur and eventually became the Chief Justice of India in 1997 through his hard work and sincerity.

In Satna, cooking was done on a chulha (traditional stove). I gradually learned the tricks of making fire in the chulha, starting with a small piece of kanda (a piece of cow dung) and adding wooden logs to it while blowing air with phookni (a utensil used to blow air). There were two chulhas side by side, functioning like two burners on a gas stove. Only rotis were cooked directly on the chulha, while other dishes like dal, sabzi, and chawal (rice) were prepared in round vessels called batua and kept on slow fire for hours to enhance their taste.

During evenings, we would cook food on a sigadi (a smaller stove) mostly in the aangan since it was very hot inside during the summer. In those days, apart from vegetables, we would prepare many other dishes from besan (gram flour) like rassaj, dhoka, meenja, and kabab from mung dal. Mung dal and urad dal baddiya were also made instead of vegetables. Food was mostly cooked in peetal (brass) utensils on which kalai (tinning) had to be done from time to time.

During that time, the popular toothpaste was Monkey Chaap Kala Dant Manjan, later replaced by Colgate tooth powder. In Satna, many people used daatoon (neem stick) instead of a toothbrush. The commonly used soap was Red Lifebuoy, while Afghan Snow was popular among the ladies. Later on, Ponds cream became popular, and the preferred hair oil was Brahmi Amla oil or coconut oil.

Two months passed, and the month of Shravan arrived. During this time, girls would visit their maike (parents' home) to celebrate festivals like Nag Panchami and Rakhi. So, my brother came to pick me up, and I eagerly took a break and went back to Jabalpur. There, I felt free like a bird, and for one week, I indulged in eating, sleeping, and reading magazines. My interests had changed since I was pregnant, and I was trying to gather as much information as I could about child-rearing and child-related topics. Meanwhile, Baboo took me to a doctor for a check-up, and I was prescribed some vitamins for my well-being. Time passed quickly, and I had to return to Satna because it was customary to have the first delivery in the sasural (in-law's home).

So, I was back in my sasural, taking care of household chores and cooking. My husband would leave in the morning and return in the evening. During this time, my sisters also came to give me company for a few days. And finally, three days before Diwali, on Dhanteras night at 2:30 AM, a baby girl was born. The delivery took place at home with the help of Mrs. Ganguli, a gynecologist who came with a nurse and used forceps. When I heard the cry of the child and saw her, tears of joy and happiness filled my eyes. All the pain I had gone through during the night was forgotten, and my heart was filled with a different kind of joy that cannot be explained in words.

On the second day, Badi Chachi (elder aunt), Jethani Shakun Bhabhi, and others were there to help and guide me in taking care of the child, including breastfeeding. Chachi's domain was always the kitchen. The arrival of a child after 25 years brought immense happiness and joy to everyone. In the morning after delivery, I was given harrera milk mixed with dry fruits, and ordinary water was replaced with ajwain-infused boiled water for drinking. For lunch, the first thing served was rice, ghee, and buknu powder along with other food. Sithora made from gud (jaggery), gond (edible gum), and dry fruits in the form of laddoos was given as the first thing in the morning for at least one month.

On the 12th day, a puja (ritual) was performed, and my siblings, amma, baboo, and others came with sweets and a box of sithora. They brought clothes for me, the baby, and pretty frocks and woolen sets for the baby as it was winter. After much discussion, we named the baby Manjari, but soon everyone started calling her Cuckoo. From then on, for the next 40 days, a malish wali (person who gives massages) would come to give massages to both me and Cuckoo. During the day, Cuckoo would play and sleep, and at night, she would wake up at 2:30 AM and start crying. Chacha and Chachi would come running after hearing her continuous crying, and a ritual called nazar utarna would be performed, where mustard, five whole red chilies, and salt would be taken around her seven times and then thrown into the fire to ward off evil eye.

Afterward, it became difficult to sleep once the child was born. During the day, everyone would play and interact with Cuckoo, but I was the one responsible for changing her langot (cloth diaper). Days passed with the routine of household work, cooking, and looking after the baby. When she turned three months old, my brother came to take me to Jabalpur, and I was overjoyed. It was a relief from the routine household chores and a chance to rest. I finally understood why girls loved going to their maike (parent's house); it provided a break from responsibilities. Here, too, everyone was happy and excited about the baby. She was like a new toy at home, and everyone enjoyed her smiles, funny sounds, and every movement. We would clap and speak to her to make her laugh.

We performed the annaprasan (first rice-eating ceremony) of Cuckoo by feeding her kheer in a silver katori (bowl) and a silver rupee. After that, she could be given some semi-liquid food like farex and dal ka paani (lentil soup). As she continued crying, we showed her to the doctor, who suggested starting bottle milk as he believed she was crying due to hunger. So, we began feeding her with bottle milk. After some time, I returned to Satna. Back in Satna, the routine of household chores, cooking, and taking care of the baby resumed. Cuckoo was growing, and she was becoming more active and interactive. During this time, she started responding to sounds and gestures, and her expressions were a constant source of joy for everyone.

As she grew older, we introduced her to different foods gradually. Pureed fruits and vegetables became a part of her diet, and she started showing preferences for certain tastes. It was a delightful experience to watch her explore new flavors and textures.

Along with taking care of the baby, I continued to learn more about childcare and read magazines and books on the subject. I sought advice from experienced mothers and relied on their guidance to ensure Cuckoo's well-being and development. The responsibility of being a new parent came with its challenges, but the love and joy that came with it overshadowed any difficulties.

During this time, the household also adapted to the needs of a baby. Safety measures were put in place, and the house was made baby-friendly. Toys, rattles, and colorful objects were introduced to stimulate Cuckoo's senses and aid her development.

As Cuckoo turned six months old, we celebrated her half-birthday with a small gathering of family and close friends. It was a joyous occasion filled with laughter, love, and blessings for the little one.

The days passed quickly, and before we knew it, Cuckoo was a year old. Her first birthday was celebrated with great enthusiasm. The house was decorated, and a small party was organized with close family members and friends. Cuckoo's laughter and innocent expressions added an extra sparkle to the celebration.

As she continued to grow, she reached various milestones, such as taking her first steps, saying her first words, and showing her unique personality. Each achievement was cherished and celebrated by everyone around her.

Looking back, those early days of motherhood in Satna hold a special place in my heart. The love, support, and joy that surrounded Cuckoo's arrival created memories that would last a lifetime. It was a period of growth, learning, and immense happiness as we embraced the journey of parenthood and witnessed the miracle of a child's growth and development.

Meanwhile, a bungalow that was under construction in Civil Lines got completed, and in 1966, we shifted to our own house. The bungalow was quite comfortable, with two bedrooms, a hall, and a large drawing room, which also served as Chacha's office as he practiced law at that time. On one side, there were racks filled with law books, Chacha's table, and chair. Chacha had planted some plants all around the boundary wall of the house. At the back, there was an aangan (courtyard) with two toilets. One of the main attractions of the house for me was a spacious open terrace. In the evenings, I could enjoy the cool breeze without having to cover my head. During summers, we would even sleep outside on cots with mosquito nets under the open sky.

During those times, table fans were common, but one or two were not enough to combat the intense heat. Hand fans were a lifesaver, and we had to use them constantly. Fans came in attractive and different designs.

Our house was named "Laxmi Shobha," after Saas-Bahu. The court was conveniently located within walking distance, which was beneficial for Chacha. However, my husband still had to cycle to the factory for work.

Since the court was nearby, Suresh Bhai Sahib, who was also a lawyer, and Bade Chacha would often visit whenever they were free. Most of the major festivals were celebrated at their house. I particularly remember the grand Holi celebrations. We would have a large houda (water tank) in the courtyard filled with colored water. After smearing each other with gulal (colored powder), we would throw colored water and dunk everyone in the houda. The colors used during Holi were sometimes difficult to remove, and it would take weeks to completely get rid of them. On Holi, we would cook special dishes like mutton with dal, bhari puri (stuffed puris), salty boiled channa dal, and moong or urad dal kachori.

Other festivals like Bhai Dooj were also celebrated at their house since all the sisters would gather together.

The more, the merrier. Lallan Bhaiya and Bhabhi would also come from Rewa, so there was always a good gathering for all the festivals.

When Cuckoo was around 11 months old and could walk a little, we performed her mundan ceremony, which had to be done within the first year. My siblings also came with lehenga chunari (traditional dress) and toys and balloons for Cuckoo. It was a joyful occasion, and her mundan ceremony was celebrated with great enthusiasm.

Next year when we celebrated her secondbirthday,I invited my husband's friends from the factory and threw a party. Chacha was not in favor of blowing candles, so we had an Indian-style celebration with gulab jamuns, gulgula (sweet fritters), and malpua.

On our next trip to Jabalpur, Baboo planned an outing for us to Pachmarhi, our first trip after marriage. He had booked a guest house for three days, and we traveled by train to Hoshangabad and then to Pachmarhi. Pachmarhi is a beautiful place with stunning scenic beauty, developed by the British like many other hill stations. We would have our meals at the guest house, but most of the time, we would venture out after brunch and return in the evening after enjoying the beauty of the Satpura Range, gardens, and various viewpoints. One of the points was Rajendra Prasad Sunset Point, which was frequently visited by Dr. Rajendra Prasad, our first president. Only the problem we faced during the trip was carrying Cuckoo, who was around 2 years old and couldn't walk much. Private cars were the primary mode of transportation there.

It was a memorable outing that refreshed us before returning to our routine after staying in Jabalpur for a few days break. Another memorable trip I recall was to Maihar, a place near Satna, known for its famous temple of Sharada Devi. To have the darshan (sight) of the goddess, one had to climb about 1000 steps. Maihar was also famous for its music gharana (school) and the presence of the renowned sarod and sitar player, Baba Allauddin Khan. Every year, a Sangeet Mahotsav (Music Festival) was held at night. Dr. Jain, our family doctor and a friend, had obtained passes for the program and invited us to join. We prepared snacks and took Cuckoo's milk bottle with us. We reached there in his car, and a grand pandal (tent) was set up for the event. Pandit Ravi Shankar, a world-renowned sitar player and Baba's disciple, was the main attraction that day. He was accompanied by the famous tabla player, Ustad Allarakha. Another highlight was the orchestra conducted by 90-year-old Baba Allauddin Khan himself, supervising all the musicians with a stick in his hand. It was a memorable scene, and we thoroughly enjoyed the program.

In 1967, my husband purchased a blue Rajdoot motorcycle. I still remember it vividly because we had many adventures on that bike. We would make Cuckoo sit in front on the tank, and on weekends, we would mostly go to Rewa as Lallan Bhaiya was there. We would say we were going to his place, but our first stop would always be the movie theater, and then we would visit his place.

Meanwhile, my husband applied for a job at Bharat Heavy Electricals Limited (BHEL) in Haridwar and got it. Chacha and Chachi were very upset about the news of us leaving, especially Chachi, who had grown attached to Cuckoo. However, in a job, you can't stay in one place for too long, so my husband joined the job in June 1968. He arranged a house for us, and after a few months, we moved there.

PART 5

A New City Brings New Life to the Family - 1968 To 1973 at Haridwar

After moving to Haridwar, it was the first time we were living on our own, away from the joint family, and we were excited about it. We carried two big metal trunks filled with clothes, a large hold-all, some kitchen utensils, a stove, and a bag containing essential cooking ingredients like flour, lentils, and rice. My husband had rented a one-bedroom house in the main city.

In a few days, I put the two boxes together and turned them into a deewan by placing a mattress on top. We also purchased four cane modhas (low stools) and a central table, which became our drawing room furniture. We bought two large beds for the bedroom a few weeks later. We got those beds for 150 rupees, and they are still with us, although we have replaced some parts and replaced the woven rope with plywood. During the purchase of the beds, my husband met a man named Rajan Bhatiya, who had a tent house business nearby. They became good friends in a short time.

Unfortunately, at that time, we couldn't get a quarter in the BHEL colony, so we had to stay in a rented house in the city. Many other friends, including Bannerji and Pathak, were also living nearby.

Haridwar is a significant pilgrimage site in the northern part of India, believed to be the abode of Lord Vishnu. Millions of people visit Haridwar throughout the year to take a dip in the holy Ganga River. The Kumbh Mela, a major Hindu festival, is also held here every 12 years. After a few days, we went to witness the Ganga Aarti (evening prayer ceremony) at Har Ki Pauri. There was a massive crowd gathered on the riverbanks, with people lighting small oil lamps and setting them afloat on leaf bowls (dona) in the river. The sight of floating lamps was beautiful. As the evening aarti began, the crowd on both sides of the river grew even larger. The priests held large fire bowls, rang bells at the temples situated on the ghats, chanted mantras, and sang the aarti. It was a mesmerizing view. Afterward, we had puri bhaji (deep-fried bread with potato curry) at one of the shops in the alleys.

Our next visit was to Rishikesh, another holy city situated near Haridwar. Rishikesh is known for its well-maintained ashrams, and the Ganga ghats there are cleaner and less crowded compared to Har Ki Pauri. We visited Parmarth Ashram, and there was a large shop called Geetabhavan next to it. Inside the shop, we found good-quality handloom bed covers at reasonable prices, and we also purchased a small copy of the Bhagavad Gita. We bought bed covers and towels at affordable rates as well.

After that, we took a bath in the Ganga and visited Laxman Jhula, a famous suspension bridge in Rishikesh. Near Muni Ki Reti, there was a restaurant called Choti Walla, where a big boy with a traditional hairstyle (choti) and wearing a dhoti stood outside to attract customers. We had vegetarian food there.

This was our first trip, and afterward, we visited Haridwar, Rishikesh, and other places several times with friends and relatives. We would bring our own food, such as puri bhaji, and during summers, we would bring mangoes and lychees, which we would dip in the cold Ganga water. By the time we finished bathing and eating, the fruits would become refreshingly cold.

Our landlady in Haridwar was an elderly Gujarati lady. In the city, non-vegetarian food was not allowed, but we would bring eggs from outside the city, and sometimes we would cook non-vegetarian dishes by closing the doors. My husband would dispose of the eggshells and bones in packets while going to the factory. Later, the landlady became suspicious and would ask Cuckoo what we had eaten.

As Rajan Bhatiya was from Dehradun, he invited us to his home one weekend. We started early on our two-wheeler and passed through Sahasradhara Falls, which is famous for its sulfur springs, on our way to Dehradun. We wandered around Paltan Bazar and finally reached his home—a loving and affectionate Punjabi business family. They warmly welcomed us, and we enjoyed a dinner of hot tandoori roti, dal, and vegetables.

The next morning, while returning after having a breakfast of parathas, Rajan's mother gave a packet of dry fruits to Cuckoo, which contained pine nuts (chilgoza), walnuts (akhrot), cashews (kaju), and more. During those times, walnuts were inexpensive, and we could get them by the kilo in Haridwar. We also had access to other fruits like litchis and apples, which were abundant during the season.

Our next trip, the following week with Bhatiya, was to Mussoorie. Bhatiya rode his scooter while we rode our Rajdoot. However, the Rajdoot couldn't handle all three of us, so we decided to exchange vehicles. Bhatiya took the Rajdoot, and we exchanged it for his Vespa to reach Mussoorie. There are several famous points in Mussoorie, including Lal Tibba, Gun Hill Point, the Company Garden, and the house of the renowned writer Ruskin Bond. We visited some of these points that day and strolled along Mall Road before returning in the evening. We made many more trips to Mussoorie afterward, with friends and relatives, enjoying the beauty of the place time and again.

During the next weekend, we went to the Mahesh Yogi Ashram in Rishikesh on our two-wheelers. Mahesh Yogi was a famous guru known for his meditation techniques. He hailed from a Kayastha family in Madhya Pradesh. At that time, he was entertaining a group of foreigners dressed in white robes. We took a round of the ashram, which had a huge and beautiful campus, and then returned. Mahesh Yogi was famous for teaching the Beatles, and there was even a university named after him. However, like most swamis, he later shifted to America.

During the day, I worked on some oil paintings on wooden frames made by a carpenter to decorate our house. Knitting sweaters was also necessary as it was very cold in Haridwar. I made many sweaters with multicolored designs, including polo necks, leggings, caps, scarves, and more for Cuckoo. I also purchased a long coat for myself to fulfill the requirement. My husband already had one. The following week, we visited Roorkee, which was only an hour or so away from BHEL. Many of us would go there for lunch. There was a famous restaurant called Polaris. Although our BHEL club was also excellent with a swimming pool, library, sports facilities, and even open-air movie screenings on weekends, we enjoyed watching movies there in the winter and summer.

Meanwhile, my husband's college classmate, Mr. Bannerji, was allotted a quarter in the BHEL colony. As he was a bachelor and a kind-hearted person, he himself shifted to another friend, Mr. Pathak's quarter, and gave his quarter to us. So, we relocated to the BHEL colony. BHEL stands for Bharat Heavy Electricals Limited, and it is located in Ranipur, a township in Haridwar. The township has its own schools, shopping center, hospital, club, bank, and post office, so there was no need to go anywhere else. It had its own charm. Here, a group was formed Pathak, Bannerji, Sajid, and my husband and our families. For evening tea and dinner, we would mostly gather at one place and enjoy all the festivals, including Eid, where Mrs. Sajid, Shakeela, would prepare delicious keema samosas, sewai, and biryani.

In the meantime, we also visited Satna. Since there was no direct train from Haridwar to Satna, we had to travel via Allahabad and change trains there. Gomati Jijji, my husband's eldest sister, used to live in Allahabad. They had a large ancestral bungalow and a joint family that was always filled with relatives. Whenever we visited Satna, we would spend the night at their place. Jijji had four daughters and two sons, and her eldest daughter, Munni, became very friendly with me. Chacha and Chachi would also stay there for a few days whenever they visited, and they enjoyed their time there. Chachi was particularly happy to visit Har Ki Pauri and Laxman Jhula, as they were famous pilgrimage sites. It was her first time visiting, and it left a lasting impression on her. She noticed that many of my friends had short hair and gave me a strict warning not to cut my hair.

Our Rajdoot was being put to good use. Our next trip was to Delhi. At that time, my cousin Madhuri Jia and her husband B.L. Jija lived in Laxmi Bai Nagar, Delhi. We went to Delhi on the 25th of January to watch the Republic Day parade on the 26th. Watching the parade live was a popular craze back then. We reached Delhi early because we had to wake up early the next day. The next morning, we all left home so that we could secure a good place to get a clear view of the parade. We didn't have VIP passes, but we managed to find a good spot where we spread our dari (mat).

Republic Day is celebrated to mark the day when the Constitution of India came into effect. The parade takes place at Rajpath, starting from Rashtrapati Bhavan and ending at India Gate. It is one of the longest and most important parades. It begins with the flag hoisting ceremony by the President. I remember that Zakir Hussain was the President at that time. The parade includes marching from various regiments of the army, navy, and air force. Tableaus from various states, depicting their culture, are also displayed. We watched the parade for some time and then returned, as it runs for a very long duration. Even while returning, we had to walk quite a lot, but it was a wonderful experience.

Whenever any guest used to come to Haridwar, we would borrow scooters from each other among our group of friends. If someone knew how to ride, it made sightseeing much easier. Bannerji got married late and so was always available with a scooter. He was a very helpful and jolly person, always cracking jokes.

In February, my sister Bina got married to Ajay Varma, who hailed from Kanpur. The wedding took place in Kanpur as per their preference, even though Ajay was working in BHEL Bhopal. Meanwhile, Baboo was transferred to Nagpur, so our next visit was to Nagpur.

We arrived in Nagpur during the summer. Bade bhaiya (elder brother) was working in the Ordnance Factory, Harish was studying engineering in Jabalpur but was here for the holidays, Usha was pursuing her M.A. in Political Science, and Anoop was in college. We stayed in a very big and beautiful bungalow. In front of the bungalow, there was a small water spring surrounded by a round chabutra (platform). At the back, there were two servant quarters where a lady named Bai stayed and a man who took care of various tasks. During the nights, we all slept outside, with cots laid out and covered with mosquito nets due to the summer season.

On one side, there was a place where vegetables were being grown, along with some fruit trees. At the back yard, there was a big wooden plank swing (jhula) for adults, where Baboo would sit in the evening. The rest of us would enjoy sitting there as well.

Nagpur is a large city and also a political center in the Vidarbha region of Maharashtra. It has a mix of Maharashtra and Madhya Pradesh cultures. Nagpur is known as the city of oranges. Our bungalow was located near Sadar Bazaar, the heart of the city. We visited local places like Ambazari Lake and enjoyed Dinshaw ice cream parlor in Sadar, which was famous at that time. We explored more local attractions as well.

Next, Baboo planned a trip to Tadoba. This time, an entire first-class railway bogie was allotted for our stay. Tadoba is located in the Chandrapur district, about 150 kilometers from Nagpur. It is a wildlife sanctuary. First, we went to Chandrapur, where a railway guest house was already booked. From there, we went for a night safari. Although tigers and leopards were present, we only spotted some deer and bears, as far as I can remember. Nonetheless, it was a nice outing. Afterward, we returned to Nagpur and enjoyed some more holidays before heading back to Haridwar.

On another trip to Nagpur, we visited Aurangabad. We stayed at Hotel Nataraj and from there, along with Cuckoo, we visited Daulatabad Fort. It was situated at a height, but all of us, including Cuckoo, managed to climb it. We also visited Bibi ka Maqbara, a shrine styled like the Taj Mahal. The following day, we went to visit the Ajanta and Ellora Caves. The Ellora Caves house the largest rock-cut Hindu temple, with many caves depicting Lord Shiva and various Hindu gods. We visited a few caves but got tired due to the extensive walking involved. Next, we explored the Ajanta Caves, which were adorned with beautiful paintings on rock-cut sculptures, depicting emotions through gestures.

After spending five days exploring these caves, we returned to Nagpur and then back to Haridwar.

During one of our visits to Satna, we also went to Bhopal for two days, where Bina and Ajay were staying. They were also residing in the BHEL colony, and our common connection was BHEL. Bhopal is a beautiful place in Madhya Pradesh. We visited the famous Birla Mandir temple of Laxmi Narain, situated at a great height, providing a panoramic view of the city. There are two famous lakes, Upper Lake and Lower Lake, which enhance the city's beauty.

Meanwhile, our friend Bhatiya was getting married, so we traveled to Dehradun to attend his Punjabi wedding, full of fun and dancing. Coincidentally, his wife was from Bombay, and her name was Padma. She was crazy about Coca-Cola and would always have two bottles whenever we were out roaming in the city. So, I always remember her whenever I have a cold drink.

In the span of one year, from 1968 to 1969, we traveled to many places, including two visits to Delhi and multiple trips to Mussoorie. We explored numerous new places. By then, I was pregnant with my second child. Meanwhile, our Rajdoot motorcycle, which we had used for all these travels, was replaced with a second-hand Lambretta scooter.

Now it was January 1970, and my second daughter was due to be born in the first week of February. My mother (Amma) was scheduled to come for the delivery on February 2nd. On January 26th, we had a dinner party at the club, which I thoroughly enjoyed, as always. On the morning of January 28th, as I was not feeling well, I went for a checkup with my husband on the scooter. The doctor advised me to get admitted immediately. Amma was informed and arrived two days later. My immediate neighbor, Mrs. Goyal, packed my bag and sent it with my husband, providing great help. She also took care of Cuckoo during that time. On that day, at 3:45 PM, my second daughter Leena was born through normal delivery. She weighed 6 pounds, and I felt happy having a glimpse of her, forgetting all the labor pain and proudly embracing motherhood for the second time.

The next day, many friends visited me with their wives, most of them newly married. They were fascinated by the baby and made comments about her cuteness, thick hair, and slender fingers. I smiled while hearing their remarks. Leena arrived earlier than expected. Another neighbor, Mrs. Srivastava, who lived downstairs, took charge of my meals and sent me harira (a traditional sweet dish) and kheer (dry fruit pudding) until Amma arrived the next day. Neighbors were always helpful, and it felt like a close-knit community.

The next day, Amma arrived and took charge of everything. On the third day, I was back home as everything was normal. Amma came fully prepared, bringing new clothes, a sweater for the new baby, a frock for Cuckoo, and a new sari for me. After 12 days, we had a Satyanarayan puja and named her Leena, as we wanted a short name. Because we were still calling Manjari "Cuckoo." Amma then took charge of me and Leena, making sithora and gond ladoo, among other things. Amma stayed with us for two months, taking care of me.

After two months, my younger sister Usha came to visit after finishing her exams. After a few days, I moved to Nagpur with Amma and the children for a few days. During that time, Leena was being lullabied by her grandmother (nani) and aunt (mausi).

After one month, when I returned, Leena was now three months old and manageable for me. My husband had been allotted our own quarter in Sector 5B. So far, we had been staying in the Bannerji house. We shifted to our own house and had a party there to celebrate Leena's birth and our new house. Our new flat was the same size as the earlier one, with two bedrooms, a balcony, and a drawing room. The location was also very good, with a shopping center opposite where we could get all our groceries and vegetables.

Downstairs, there was Mr. Jagmohan, whose wife Karuna became my very good friend in a few days. They had a daughter named Parul, who was the same age as Cuckoo, so they became classmates and friends, going to BHEL school together on the bus.

Karuna was very friendly with Leena too, and they became attached to each other.

Mr. Vijay Dadoo, who was a close friend of theirs, also became a close friend of ours. Mr. Dadoo had gotten married at that time, and his wife Prabha also became a very good friend of mine. Another family, Mr. and Mrs. Tripathi, also joined our group of friends, forming a group of four families. We would go on holidays together, ride our two-wheelers, and have dinners or tea at each other's houses. There was always some occasion to celebrate, like marriage anniversaries and birthdays.

Meanwhile, my eldest brother got married in December 1970 when Leena was 11 months old. We went to Nagpur and then joined the wedding procession by train with friends and relatives to Datia, a town in Madhya Pradesh where the bride's father was posted. We enjoyed playing cards and chatting on the train. In Datia, we visited temples and enjoyed the hospitality and food. Afterward, we returned to Nagpur, where there was a warm reception for local friends and relatives. We also met Prem Baboo, who was working in Nagpur and would later become Usha's husband. Their marriage was fixed for February 1971.

Our next visit in February was to Lucknow, where Usha's wedding was to take place at Shanta Mausi's house. Amma's cousin lived there, and though our house at the back was not fully ready, we enjoyed the wedding, eating delicacies of Lucknow, including the famous malai paan. We also met many relatives from Amma's side of the family.

Leena was gradually growing up and learning new things every day. She was very talkative and would call herself "Eena" when she couldn't speak properly. When Mr.Jagmohan would take out his scooter, she would say, "Uncle, cooter, Eena dar." We still remember this sentence after so many years. When Cuckoo went to school, she would take her lunchbox and water bottle and go to Karuna's house for some time, saying, "I am going to school."

When she turned two years old, we performed her Mundan (hair shaving ceremony). She would stand in front of the mirror and sing, "Ganju Patel, teri khopdi mein tail, ek danda maru chal padi rail." She was quite the nautanki (dramatic) and chatterbox.

In December 1971, there was a war between India and Pakistan. It was actually the Bangladesh Liberation War in East Pakistan, which lasted from December 3rd to December 16th. Due to BHEL's proximity to the border, precautions were taken. Our flat windows were covered with black paper, and patrolling was done at night by 5 to 6 people from the colony for safety. My husband would also participate in the patrolling. It was a different experience, and thankfully, it ended in 15 days.

In the colony, many people would come out for a walk after dinner and enjoy paan (betel leaf). We would join them, eat paan, have some gupshup (chit-chat), and then return home. During the summer vacations, we went to Shimla, a hill station in Himachal Pradesh. We traveled by a night bus that reached in the morning. Shimla was a very beautiful hill station with colorful houses up and down the hills. We roamed on Mall Road and Ridge Road, which was an open space for social activities. Shimla was a lively hill station with many things happening during the summer. We enjoyed a delicious Punjabi lunch and returned the next morning. Unfortunately, it was raining, so we could only enjoy the view from our room and couldn't go out for long.

Time passed, and during Diwali, we went to Satna to visit Chachi, who was not in very good health. Chacha also had an eye problem with glaucoma and cataract. The doctor had recommended surgery, but he was not ready for it. He was still practicing with the help of an assistant who would transcribe his dictated cases. Jogeswar, a man who had worked under my husband in Satna, was now staying with Chacha and Chachi in our house, taking care of them. He was a very dedicated man and served them till the end.

At Satna with my in-laws

We came back, and in the colony, Prabha also had a baby girl named Rachana. My pastime activities were knitting and reading novels whenever I got some free time. During that time, I read novels by Sharad Chandra and Prem Chandra. Gulshan Nanda was also very popular for Hindi novels at that time, and some of his novels were even made into movies, like "Kati Patang."

During Cuckoo's summer holidays, I went with the children to Nagpur to spend the holidays. My husband was still in Haridwar. Madhu Bhabhi was also there for her first delivery, and Usha had come to Nagpur after having her delivery in Lucknow. We had a great time together. After a month, on June 20th, we received news from Satna that Chachi had passed away due to a brain hemorrhage. Anoop was there, so I, along with the children, proceeded to Satna by bus. As soon as I left for Satna, Bhabhi Ji went to the hospital, and the next day, Roopesh, their first child, was born.

My husband also reached Satna from Haridwar, but since there was no direct train, he had to change trains, and by the time he reached, Lallan Bhaiya had already performed the last rites, as the body couldn't be kept due to the hot summer weather. Everyone, including Badi Chachi, Bhabhi, and all the cousins who were local, werealready there. Gomati Jijji also came. On the third day, we took the ashes to Allahabad for visarjan (immersion), and then the terhavi (rituals on the thirteenth day) were performed.

Now Chacha also had to wind up gradually as he couldn't live alone in Satna. During our next visit, the house was rented to an advocate named Mr. Vijay

Singh, and one room was locked with some belongings. Houses are built with so much care and hard work, as if we are going to live there forever, but ultimately, you never know how long you will stay. Chacha reluctantly shifted with us afterward, as it was difficult for him to adjust to flat and colony life compared to his previous bungalow. Many times, he would stay in Allahabad at Gomati Jijji's place, where he was well taken care of.

After a few days, we took him to the Sitapur Eye Hospital, a renowned hospital for glaucoma and cataract surgeries, but the doctor said it was too late, and his eyesight was deteriorating. After a few more days, Bade Bhaiya also joined BHEL, and Roopesh was a few months old. So we started going on picnics and outings together. We sold our old black Ford car and purchased a second-hand Ambassador car of light green color.

We settled nicely in BHEL with good friends, colony life, and our house set up. However, at the end of 1972, my husband had already applied for a new job in HAL (Hindustan Aeronautics Limited) in Nasik and got an appointment letter. He had to join in October 1973. After five years in Haridwar, we had to shift again, but this time with two daughters and Chacha. It was not an easy task. After staying outside Maharashtra for ten years, five years in Madhya Pradesh and five years in Uttar Pradesh, I was moving back to Maharashtra, where I had grown up.

We were going to miss friends like Dadoo and Banerjee, who are still our friends, along with many others. Most of the furniture we had purchased in BHEL was second-hand and was sold. We kept only some important things and transported them to Jhansi, where Baboo was posted and had a big bungalow. It was time to bid farewell to all my friends, but I carried wonderful memories of the BHEL township with me as we started our journey to Jhansi.

We came by car, first to Agra, where Baboo joined us. We stayed at the railway guest house in Agra and visited the famous Taj Mahal in the morning with Baboo, Chacha, and all of us. Then we went to Jhansi. My husband left us and the car in Jhansi and joined his new job in Nasik, Maharashtra, at HAL Ozar township.

After some time, when he settled in the quarter, he came to pick us up, and again by car, we started our journey to Nasik, with a break journey in Bhopal for one day, where Bina and Ajay were staying. Finally, we reached Nasik, the HAL Ozar township.

PART 6

Moving Away From Our Comfort Zones -1973 To1977 at Ozar near Nashik

Finally, we reached our new destination, H.A.L. Ozar, in our ambassador loaded with lots of luggage. H.A.L. stands for Hindustan Aeronautics Ltd. It manufactures fighter jets, helicopters.

The colony was self-equipped, like B.H.E.L., having everything: a school, shopping center, club, theater, etc. Our quarter was on the ground floor. The pattern of the house was the same as B.H.E.L., with two bedrooms, a balcony, a drawing room, and a kitchen. The rooms were slightly smaller. Opposite our building was an open ground, followed by the H.A.L. High School for children, a shopping center, and a dispensary. Everything was nearby, which was a big relief for me.

As we settled, our immediate neighbor, the Seshashayis', a hospitable South Indian family, offered us coffee. They had two children, Prasad and Keshav. Living upstairs were Mr. and Mrs. Dekhane, a Maharashtrian family, and next to them were Mr. Pai Angle, and his family. Mr. Pai Angle was the principal of the H.A.L. school. We had a good cosmopolitan neighborhood.

The next task was to get Manjari, my elder daughter who was in 3rd grade, admitted to school. There was no problem with that, except that it was December and half the session was already over. So she had to work hard, but the teachers and her friends were very cooperative. Leena, my younger daughter, also joined in lower KG.

The furniture, including a sofa, cupboard, table, fan, and sewing machine from my marriage that were lying idle in Satna, were transported here. In a few days, we settled into our new home. Here, my husband was very busy in the factory for the first 2 years, hardly getting any time for the family. So I had to look after everything: the children's health, studies. And now, Chacha, my father-in-law who had gone to Allahabad for a few days, was also back. He was very particular about food and its timings, making my life even busier.

The club and theater were there, but we hardly got time for anything in the first 2 years.

Gradually, the Ganotras', Indoriyas', and Prasads, as well as the Maliks became our friends. During Janmashtami, we were introduced to Mr. V.P. Agrawal, who was working at Indian Oil Corporation. In due course, we also became close friends with the Agrawals. Mrs. Agrawal, who was from an army family was very particular and perfect in everything. They had two daughters, Poonam and Naina (Chotu). Poonam was Leena's classmate. We started enjoying weekends and birthdays at each other's places. Birthdays were particularly fun, as everything, from cakes to other preparations, were made at home. So, the preparations would start a day before. I would stitch new dresses at home for the girls, and my sewing machine was used to its full capacity, even for stitching other needs for the home.

Gradually, we went for some sightseeing in Nasik, visiting temples like Mukti Dham, Panchvati, Sita Gupha, Kala Ram Temple, Someshwar Temple, and the Godavari River and Godavari Temple. As we settled down after a few months, we went to Shirdi in a car with Mr. Agrawal and his family. Shirdi is a famous temple dedicated to Sai Babaji, who is revered as a saint and fakir. Anyone who visited us would go to Shirdi for sure.

Our next trip was to Trimbakeshwar, which is believed to be the place of origin of river Ganga. At that time, it was not as crowded as it is now, and we could easily get darshan.

Janmashtami (Lord Krishna's birthday) was celebrated by inviting close family friends. Jhanki (decorations depicting incidents from Krishnaji's life) and prasad (sacred food offering) were prepared. It was great fun for the children, with dancing and singing. I would be busy making prasad for everyone, and as we used to have a fast on that day, some special delicacies would also be made. Upon returning to Maharashtra, we also celebrated Makar Sankranti and Ganesh Chaturthi in a grand way.

Manjari had a good exposure to drawing in school. She joined elementary drawing classes, took exams, and ranked among the top 30 students in Maharashtra. Her photo appeared in the newspaper, and we were overjoyed. Her interest in drawing started from there. Mr. Sahdeo, a very good drawing teacher, was also a good motivator.

In February 1975, Harish got married. As Baboo was posted in Jhansi at that time, we went to Jhansi for the wedding. From there, the wedding procession went to Allahabad because Manjula, his wife, is from Allahabad. Many relatives and cousins had gathered in Allahabad for the marriage. Afterward, we returned to Jhansi and visited Jhansi Fort, bringing back childhood memories as I had spent my childhood there. We also visited our old house and met some relatives. Baboo was going to retire in a few months, as the retirement age in government jobs at that time was 56. Five of his children were settled and married, except for Anoop, who was yet to get married. We enjoyed spending time with all our siblings and relatives, some of whom we hadn't seen in a long time. We returned home after a few days.

During those days, we used to purchase wheat in bulk and store it in a large drum. Whenever we needed flour, I had to clean the wheat and put it in a canister, then take it for grinding to a flour mill. Vegetables were also bought on Sundays from the wholesale market and stored. Onions were very cheap, around 2 rupees per kilogram, in Nasik during that time. Grapes were also very cheap when they were in season.

Our neighbor, Mrs. Pai Angle, who was from Goa, used to visit our house frequently. She told me that in Goa, cats were considered very lucky, and many households had cats as pets. There was a pregnant cat that used to roam around those days. Mrs. Pai Angle made arrangements for the cat's delivery at her home, with cushions and all, and used to feed her. However, the cat ended up giving birth to four lovely kittens in our house cupboard. Now, Mrs. Pai Angle would come to our house with milk for the kittens and feed them. She said that something very good would happen to us. I didn't believe in such things, but coincidentally, I conceived in February, and my husband, who had applied for a job, received a very good offer from M.I.C.O. in Nasik.

Before joining the new job, we went to Mahabaleshwar for a three-day outing, which was long overdue after the children's exams. We stayed in a hotel near the Indian Oil guest house, where Mr. Agrawal and his family had arranged accommodation. We spent the whole day together, exploring the beautiful points in Mahabaleshwar, such as Arthur Seat. The children enjoyed playing in the park. We had a great time eating cone ice cream and ice gola. The strawberry season was coming to an end, and we purchased honey, jams, and other famous products from there. On the way back, we bought chikki and chiwda from Lonavala. It was a good trip.

This time, shifting was easier as we had to move from Ozar to Nasik city. The company provided moving & packing charges, and we moved into a bungalow this time, and not a flat. So, 1977 started on a good note for us, and we shifted to Nasik City.

PART 7

To New Friendships and a New Addition - 1977 To 1987 at Nashik

So, here we were in S.B.I. Colony, M.I.C.O., Nasik city. After 8 years of staying in a flat, we got an opportunity to stay in a bungalow, which was very comfortable. It had a big drawing cum dining hall, two bedrooms, a kitchen, and an open balcony. In front of the bungalow, there was a large yard, which we used for gardening, and there was a big mango tree on the left side. At the back, there were many papaya and banana trees. We had Mr. C.N.S. Rao, staying in the upstairs unit with his wife and two children, Sriram and Laxmi. Across the road, there were hutments, where many of the servants coming to the colony would stay. We had the convenience of having a maid servant, who also stayed there.

Our neighbors were friendly. As we settled in the evening, Mrs. Rao offered us filter coffee with snacks. The Asthana's our immediate neighbors, and we were invited by Mrs. Asthana for dinner. The Asthana family of Sundar Asthana, Poonam, and their daughter Guddi were our immediate neighbors in the next unit. The next agenda was to get school admission for Cuckoo and Leena. Both of them were admitted to Nirmala Convent High School, with Cuckoo in 7th grade and Leena in 3rd grade. Many children from the colony also attended the same school, and the school bus would come to pick them up.

For medical needs, we had to choose private doctors since there was no hospital nearby, similar to our experience in BHEL. We selected Dr. Pandit as our family doctor and Dr. Pawar as the gynecologist for my delivery. We also found a good maid servant named Chabi, who stayed nearby. Janmashtami arrived, and we celebrated it with decorations and jhanki. I invited all the society ladies and children for prasad in the evening. Mrs. Rao helped me in making prasad, and she made a full parat (a large plate) of coconut barfi for distribution. It had a different flavor with a touch of South Indian taste as she added some kapur (camphor) to it. This became a regular feature every year, and we continue to celebrate Janmashtami on a smaller scale even now.

The Kudwas' and the Sahis', two more families from the colony, became very friendly with us in a few days. Mrs.

Kudwa had three sons named Vishu, Vivek, and Vinnu, and Mrs. Sahi had three children named Maneesh, Reema and Sonu. In the colony, we used to have potluck dinners where each lady would make one dish, resulting in a variety of food, especially South Indian dishes.

We enjoyed the festivities of Ganpati, where different competitions were held for children. After Dussehra, on 30th October, we celebrated Karwa Chauth, the only festival during which I used to fast apart from Janmashtami. The due date given by the doctor for my delivery was 10th November. My mother arrived on the 1st of November. On Karwa Chauth night, I kept a fast with phalahar (eating only fruits and certain food items allowed during fasting). After performing the puja of the moon and having dinner, I started feeling uncomfortable with slight pain. We decided to go to the hospital, leaving Cuckoo, who was now 11 years old, behind.

The next morning, at 5:30 a.m., a cute baby boy weighing 7 pounds was delivered. It was a normal delivery, and as soon as the nurse showed me the baby, I forgot all the pain I had gone through during the night and was filled with joy at the sight of my healthy and adorable baby. My husband and Chacha were overjoyed to hear the news of a male child, which they had been longing for. Pedhas (a sweet) were distributed in the colony as per the custom in Maharashtra. I stayed in the hospital for 5 days and then came back home.

My mother stayed with us for about a month, taking care of me before returning to Lucknow, where they had settled after retirement.

On the 12th day, we performed the customary Satyanarayan Puja. After much discussion, we chose the name Anubhav, as names starting with 'A' were popular at that time. However, we started calling him Mintoo as a nickname, which is still used today. Amma stayed with us for about a month and took care of me, leaving behind a good stock of sithora (a traditional sweet) and ladoos and giving me a lot of instructions, as all mothers do.

So this Diwali was special for our family as my daughters got a brother to celebrate Bhai Dooj, which is done after Diwali. They were excited and performed the puja of Bhai Dooj. I was also happy looking at all of them enjoying and celebrating together. After a few days, we purchased a pram for Mintoo. I thought it would be more comfortable as I could take him to the kitchen while cooking and take care of him. In the evenings, we would use it for walks. After some time, we also hired Meena, the daughter of our maid servant Chabi, to look after Mintoo part-time. He was a well-behaved child who didn't give us much trouble, except that he wanted to go for walks in the evening. As he was born after a gap of 7 years, he was pampered to some extent but not spoiled. We had a big party to celebrate his first birthday.

I was always fond of music, so our transistor radio was always on most of the time, starting from the morning. Mintoo would point towards the things he needed, and his wishes would be fulfilled. As a result, he started speaking a bit later compared to Leena, who started speaking early and was very talkative.

The following year, during the Diwali holidays, we went to Lucknow to celebrate Mintoo's first birthday. My two younger brothers, Harish and Anoop, who were posted in Lucknow at that time, were also there. Harish was working in the railways (later he joined RITES), and Anoop was working at Scooters India. Harish was married to Manjula, and they had a baby girl named Mili, who was an year older than Mintoo. Manjula was a very good-natured girl. During our stay, Mili and Mintoo would play together, and coincidentally, the cousins are still very close.

As always, we enjoyed our trip. We started the day with hot jalebis that Baboo used to bring for breakfast. In the evenings, hot samosas were readily available on every corner of Lucknow. We would also indulge in chaat, non-vegetarian dishes, and rabdi at night. During the evenings, we would roam around Hazratganj or Aminabad, which were within walking distance. Sometimes we would go to the movies in a cycle rickshaw, which was a pastime back then.

Our house in Lucknow had a drawing room, three bedrooms, a dining room, a kitchen, and a courtyard with a tulsi plant. There was also a large bedroom on the terrace. Shanta Mausi used to live near our house. Sadly, Mausa ji was no longer with us, and Madhuri jia and Meera were already married. Rajeev and Anil, their sons, used to stay there. We would frequently visit their house.

Once a year, we would visit Lucknow to utilize our L.T.A. (Leave Travel Allowance), which could be used annually. The next year, when we went to Lucknow, we also visited Nainital, a beautiful hill station in the Himalayas. It was situated around Naini Lake, a popular boating site, and had the Nainadevi Temple. We stayed there for two days, enjoying a boat ride and spending time with our parents and siblings before returning to Nasik.

In Nasik, the Hindi Sabha, an organization of Hindi-speaking people that my husband joined, was very active. Especially during Holi, which was celebrated on a large scale. On the first day, Holi ka Dahan (Holi bonfire) would be arranged, and snacks and thandai (a traditional drink) would be served. The next day, we would go to play Holi at Someshwar Temple, which was on the banks of a river. We would play Holi and have lunch prepared there. We became very friendly with Mr. Tiwari and his family. They had four children: Vijay, Renu, Veenu, and Chotu. Sometimes, Hasya Kavi Sammelans (comic poetry gatherings) were organized by the Hindi Sabha during Holi, where famous poets of that time, such as Kaka Hathrasi, Shail Chaturvedi,

Ashok Chakradhar, and Hullad Muradabadi, would come to perform.

In MICO, there were many cultural activities apart from parties in the club and movies. Drama competitions were also a part of it, but at that time, all the dramas were in Marathi. Tiwari, Asthana, and some other members, including my husband, thought of starting Hindi plays. So I also started participating in them with my husband. The plays were organized on a large scale. A director was hired to teach and a place was provided for practice. Mintoo was young, but after dinner, we would take him for practice, and he would sleep on a mattress (gadda).

My husband and me in one of the plays

Glimpses of the hindi plays

From 1980 to 1987, we did many plays. It was a unique experience to perform on stage, and our children also participated in various cultural activities like plays, dance, fancy dress competitions, etc.

Apart from that, there was a Fine Art Association where exhibitions were held for employees' families. Our family would showcase craft pieces like drawings, wall hangings, paintings, embroidery, and knitting. Our family received maximum prizes for being the most creative and active in these exhibitions.

On Sports Day, Leena from our family was a star. She was a very talented athlete and a great runner in both school and MICO sports. Once in MICO sports, she came second and was the state runner-up, which was a great achievement. Some people suggested that we should train her in running as her long strides were impressive, but at that time, we didn't give much importance to such suggestions.

Meanwhile, in our society, Shobha used to teach Bharatanatyam dance. Leena started learning along with other girls from the colony. Later, she became a student of Mrs. Robins, where she performed on stage as well. During that time, she learned Alaripu and Jathiswaram in Bharatanatyam. We also purchased full jewellery for her Bharatanatyam dance, but later, due to her studies, dance took a backseat.

In 1980, we went to Lucknow for Anoop's marriage. His wife, Reeta, was from Lucknow, so it was a local marriage and the last marriage in our family. Manjula came from Allahabad, her parents' house, with their one-month-old son, Monu, who was their second child after Mili. Usha, my younger sister, also came from Hazaribagh, Bihar, where Prem Baboo was posted at that time. Like all marriages, there was a lot of fun and a gathering of relatives with dancing, singing, and a reception.

It was Cuckoo's 10th year in school, and for her, a Hercules ladies' cycle was purchased as she had to go for tuition classes. Later, Leena also used it. During the summer of that year, we went to Satna and from there to Chitrakoot, a famous pilgrimage site, for Mintoo's mundan (tonsure ceremony). He was now two and a half years old and had nice curly hair. Chitrakoot was a famous pilgrimage site associated with Lord Rama and Allahabad Wali Gomati Jijji accompanied us. Jijaji and Badi Chachi also accompanied us. Mintoo wore a

Pathan suit, which was in fashion at that time, and he looked cute in it.

The next year, Mintoo was admitted to higher KG at St. Xavier School. St. Xavier was one of the best boys' schools in Nasik Road, near Infant Jesus Church, which was very famous and still is. The next day, Mintoo came home from school and told me that there was a girl in his class who also had plaits. In the beginning, I used to accompany him to drop him off at school, and one day I saw a Sikh boy with two big plaits. He was the same girl Mintoo had mentioned. We corrected him and taught him about Sikhism.

Mintoo, although quiet and observant, was very intelligent from the beginning, just like all my children who were good and sincere in their studies. In higher KG, he topped his class, and his class teacher jokingly told him to bring barfi (a sweet) for her. But Mintoo insisted that I should give the barfi for the teacher and took it to Barna teacher, who was famous for being very strict.

When he was in 1st grade, I discovered while checking his homework that he had done a math problem correctly, but the teacher had marked it wrong. When I went to the school to enquire, the class teacher informed me that he had copied the problem incorrectly from the blackboard. We requested the teacher to make him sit in the front bench instead of the back, and we also took him to an eye specialist. It turned out that he needed glasses. We were initially upset, thinking about how such a young child would manage with glasses. But then we noticed many other children wearing glasses, and we realized that it was more common than we thought.

In the beginning, we received a lot of advice from well-wishers, suggesting things like giving him carrot juice or trying magnet therapy. I tried the magnet therapy for a while. With his big glasses, Mintoo resembled the child from the Kismi Toffee advertisement. For a mother, her child is always cute, but he surely faced some teasing from his classmates about wearing glasses.

During that time, we became close friends with Mr. U.S. Singh, who came from MICO Bangalore on deputation for three years. He had two children, Sanjay and Suman, who were the same age as Leena. He was an outgoing and jolly person, and we started going on outings and picnics together every weekend. There were many nearby places in Nasik where we could go, such as Bhandardhara and Someshwar. We also enjoyed going to the movies, and our favorite theater was KINO in H.L, Ozar. The manager there knew us well, and even if it was house full, he would arrange extra benches for us.

In 1982, the Asian Games were held in Delhi, and it was a famous event during those times. We went to Delhi to witness the games. My younger brother, Harish, lived there, and we stayed with him. Since India was the host, Delhi was fully transformed in preparation for the games. The mascot, Appu the elephant, became famous. We watched some matches on TV and some in the stadium. It was a good change, and we later visited Delhi a few more times, exploring places like the Rail Museum, India Gate, the sound and light show at the Red Fort, and many other attractions. My younger sister, Beena, was also in Delhi with Harish and other relatives.

In the meantime, as time passed, we became eligible for a three-day stay with the family at a 5-star hotel through a tie-up with the WelcomeGroup. We were given Rs. 200 food coupons per day. To avail this facility, we first went to Searock Hotel in Bombay. Having air conditioning and a TV in the room was a luxury for us during that time. We would go out in the morning, roam around, have pizza at Band Stand, go to Linking Road, eat Chinese food from street vendors, and come back in the evening. We would have dinner with soup, dinner rolls, and a rice dish so that we could use our Rs. 200 per day effectively. We had also brought some snacks from home for intermittent eating.

In Nasik, during those days, there were only two popular places to dine, Prakash Ka Dabba and Green View Hotel. For official work, my husband used to visit Bangalore frequently, and during one of those trips, we also went in 1987, using our Leave Travel Allowance (LTA). We stayed at Windsor Manor Hotel and enjoyed the luxury of the hotel. We visited many places like Lalbagh, Cubbon Park, Banargatta Park, and Vidhan

Soudha. Mr. U.S. Singh, our friend from MICO, had returned to Bangalore and settled there. They had a big house, and we also visited them.

From there, we went to Ooty and enjoyed the beautiful view of the tea plantations and other tourist spots. Going to Bangalore without shopping for sarees is impossible. So, we purchased some silk sarees from the main market. The quality of the sarees was so good that some of them are still with me after being used by my daughters for many years.

We also went to Goa once by Kadamba bus and stayed at Citade de Goa hotel. It was a very memorable stay. The 5-star hotel had its own beach where we could relax. It was our first experience of the beach, and it was unforgettable. After returning home, we continued with our usual life in the colony. In Nasik, grapes would be very cheap during the season, around Rs. 4 per kg, and there were orchards near our home. So, we would make grape juice, tomato sauce, orange juice, and pickles for the whole year. I also learned many South Indian dishes like Bisi Bele Bhat, curd rice, dosa, and fluffy idli from my South Indian friends.

Life in the colony was very relaxed. I would leave Mintoo at the school bus stop, which was in front of Mrs. Kudwa's house. All the ladies would sit together for about an hour, chatting, having coffee, and gossiping. Then, when everyone felt refreshed, we would return home and start our household chores. It was a very laid-back and enjoyable life.

In 1984, my husband and his friend Mr. Rajgopal Menon decided to purchase our own flat. A new project was being developed on College Road, so both friends booked a flat there. In 1985, the flat was ready, and we shifted there, saying goodbye to the SBI colony where we had wonderful times. Our building was named "Panama," a funny name given by the builder. Our flat was on the ground floor, and Rajgopal's was on the 3rd floor. It was a comfortable house with three bedrooms, a drawing room, and a kitchen with a small balcony where we kept some plants on the grills. The building had a total of 8 families. Our immediate neighbor was Mr. Oak on the ground floor, followed by the Jamdar, Joshi, Ranade, and Binniwale families. They all came from different backgrounds. Mr. Oak was an elderly man who used to teach tabla. Later, Mintoo and Raj Gopal's son, Nitin, learned tabla from him for a year.

Gradually, we settled into our new home and furnished it. The old black and white TV was replaced with a color TV, and the furniture was gradually replaced with new teakwood furniture. We had a huge sofa-cum-bed, a big dining table, and other furniture made to order, so they were strong and durable. They are still with us, although the upholstery has been changed many times. The following year, Cuckoo completed her BSc and got admission to an MBA program in a college on College Road. Mintoo continued studying at St. Xavier School, and his school bus would stop near our house.

My family in Nasik

In June, Leena's 10th-grade exam results were announced, and as usual, she had topped her school. To celebrate, we organized an evening party for the residents of our building. Additionally, in our small society, we would have a Kojagiri party on the terrace under the moonlight, enjoying basundi and pav bhaji while chatting and the children played. Later, the ladies of the building started a kitty party where we exchanged culinary skills. Jayshree, who was from Kerala, and I, representing North Indian dishes, were especially active in this group.

My day would start by going to the nearby milk booth with glass bottles with blue caps at 5:30 AM. The milk's quality was excellent, and I would use it to make butter and ghee at home. Everything was made from scratch at home, including sabudana papad and potato chips. Jayshree and I would visit the grinding machine to make fresh masalas for our food. There were different machines available for this purpose.

Then, on October 31, 1984, Mintoo's birthday preparations were underway for the evening party when suddenly news broke out that Indira Gandhi, the Prime Minister of India, had been assassinated at her residence on Safdarjung Road in New Delhi by her Sikh bodyguards. The news spread like wildfire, and even at the evening birthday party, the elders were busy discussing this tragic event while the children enjoyed the celebrations.

Around this time, we also became acquainted with a new family friend, Mr. Arun Varma, through our MICO friend, Mr. Saran. Arun and Sunanda had two sons, Ashish and Akshay, who were the same age as Mintoo. We became very close friends with them and have remained friends to this day. On weekends, we would go for morning walks. Our flat was near Bhosala Military School, a famous army school. The area had a lot of open space at the time, and there was a famous Ram temple where the idol was made from melted metal of used bullets by the students. However, the area has since become more crowded.

After completing her BSc, Cuckoo joined an MBA program in 1986, and Leena expressed her desire to become a doctor. She started attending biology classes using the Hercules cycle that Cuckoo had previously used. Cuckoo's college was within walking distance from our flat. Afterward, Cuckoo had to work on a project for her MBA, which required her to visit MICO Company. For this purpose, we purchased a blue-colored scooter for her. Meanwhile, I was settling into our new house, and Leena was now in 12th grade.

However, my husband decided to join a company in Pune, with the influence of his boss, Mr. Limaye. After Leena completed her 12th-grade exams, we shifted to Pune. It was decided that Cuckoo would stay in a hostel for a year, and Mr. Varma and Mr. Raj Gopal became her local guardians in our absence. We believed that Pune would offer better opportunities for Leena to pursue her medical aspirations. Thus, we finally made the move to Pune.

PART 8

The City We Decided To Call Home – 1987 to Present at Pune

We shifted to Pune, a city in Maharashtra known for its pleasant weather throughout the year. It was once the base of the Peshwas of the Maratha Empire. We fell in love with the city and decided to make it our home, and after 36 years, we're still here. Over the years, the city has transformed from a green traditional city to a cosmopolitan hub with tall buildings.

We first arrived in Pune, at Sahwas Society, Karve Nagar, in our Ambassador car. We had found a beautiful small bungalow on rent. The society mostly comprised Maharashtrian families. Since our children were brought up in Maharashtra, they studied Marathi as a subject in school and became fluent in the language. Our landlord and neighbor, Major General

Kulkarni, who had served in the army, welcomed us with great hospitality.

Our son, Mintoo, started attending Loyola School, one of the best schools in Pune. He had the opportunity to engage in swimming and sports like basketball, which provided him with good exposure. Mintoo made some wonderful friends namely Nikhil, Indy and Vishwas. Meanwhile, Leena, our daughter, received her 12th-grade results and passed with flying colors, as always. Based on her marks, she got admission to the Government Medical College in Nagpur, as becoming a doctor was her dream. Though we were excited for her, we also had concerns about ragging in medical colleges. However, having my younger sister Usha in Nagpur, provided some comfort as they became her local guardians, since she had to stay in the hostel. At the hostel, Leena made good friends and had a great room partner named Sita, whose parents treated her very well.

During our time in Pune, we were introduced to a friend named Mr. Prakash Bhalerao, who was the brother of my husband's classmate, Avinash Bhalerao, from Raipur. Prakash worked as the Vice President in Bharat Forge. Two more friends, Mr. Indoriya and Mr. Ganotra, who were in Bharat Forge in Pune and Nasik, respectively, also became part of our social circle. Mr. Indoriya was a frequent visitor and used to stay in Mitra Mandal during those times. He had two sons.

Meanwhile, my cousin Madhuri Jia, who was in Delhi, had her son join the National Defence Academy (NDA) in Khadakwasla. He would mostly visit us on weekends. Cuckoo, who at this time was in her final year of MBA, was in a hostel in Nasik. She had Jayshree and Mr. Raj Gopal, as well as Arun and Sunanda Varma, our old friends, as her local guardians. After completing her final year, she came to Pune and took up a job in Datapro- an IT consultancy firm. While she settled into her career, we continued our search for a suitable boy for her. My elder brother, Sushil, who was still working in B.H.E.L., along with Baboo, was a frequent visitor, and they suggested a boy, the son of Dr. Lal, who practiced in B.H.E.L. Eventually, everyone approved, and their marriage took place in May 1989, at Haridwar, in a lavish manner, being the first marriage in our family. Some of my old friends like Bannerji and Mr. Dadoo were there, along with my brother, and they were of great help.

By the time we returned after a few days, there was another change in my husband's job. He moved from Perfect Machine Tools, where he had initially joined, to Greaves Ltd. We also moved to a different house on Prabhat Road, an airy flat on the 3rd floor of an apartment building. The location was excellent, in one of the posh areas of Pune, surrounded by greenery. Across the road was Suvarnarekha Dining Hall, one of the best and affordable places for thalis (traditional Indian meals) during those times. The location was also convenient, as it was near Deccan Gymkhana, within walking distance of Laxmi Road, a famous sari market. Additionally, Mintoo's bus stop was just around the corner, and there was a city bus stop in front, which was a great advantage as we often traveled by bus during those times.

In the new neighborhood, I made a good friend named Suguna Rao, who lived opposite us and had three children. Since I had free time during the day, we used to roam around by bus, visiting Tulsi Bagh for shopping. Tulsi Bagh was not a garden, but the main market comprising a large wholesale vegetable market and other shops where you could find everything at wholesale rates. There was also a good bakery shop, and for me, there was Samrat Woolen House, a great shop for various types of wool at reasonable prices. Knitting was my main hobby at the time. Tulsi Bagh was like a market surrounding a temple dedicated to Lord Rama. Pune is known for its various "peths" (market areas), such as Budhwar Peth, Nana Peth, Sadashiv Peth, and Guruwar Peth. Both Mrs. Rao and I loved shopping and exploring these markets, often traveling by bus. However, we mainly bought household items and vegetables, not much for ourselves.

Baboo and Amma used to visit us regularly, at least once a year, and stay for a few days, until he was active, which was until 1997. During one of Baboo's visits, he took us to meet his friend, Mr. Joshi, who had previously worked in the railway and now had his own business. Through Mrs. Tara Joshi, I was introduced to my new kitty party friend, Mrs. Prema Gupta. Mrs. Agarwal, Mrs. Ravindranath, and many more friends also became part of our social circle. Although kitty parties have stopped due to the pandemic, we are still good friends.

Whenever Amma, Baboo, or other relatives used to come, we would visit many places like Dagdu Sheth Ganpati Temple, Parvati Temple, Aga Khan Palace, Mastani Mahal, Kelkar Museum, Shaniwar Wada, and Rajneesh Ashram in Koregaon Park. This ashram, also known as Osho ashram, is actually a meditation center. There was a galli called Osho Galli nearby where we used to get colorful chappals and robes of Rajneesh.

M.G. Road or Camp, as it was called, was a posh cosmopolitan area with good restaurants. There was a famous Irani cafe that supplied vegetarian and non-vegetarian patti samosas, and other specialties, apart from bun maska. Whenever someone would come to Pune, we would give them peda, batata chivda, and bhakarwadi from Chitale Bandhu. For relatives who had less time and wanted to visit all the places, I would take them on the Pune Darshan bus as it covered many points in a day.

Apart from local places, most visitors would also go to Shirdi, the famous Sai Baba temple. Some would also visit Mahabaleshwar, Lonavala, and Khandala. Watching films was also a major pastime for entertainment. Alka Talkies was a well-located theater for us. Hotel Blue Diamond was considered the first 5-

star hotel, and Vaishali on Ferguson College Road was famous for its South Indian dishes. Speaking of which, Ferguson College is one of the oldest colleges, nearly 100 years old.

Pune being a center of education, many relatives' children would come to study here. My cousin Madhuri's son, Puneet, used to come on weekends, and now Meera's son has also joined the NDA. Let me tell you more about the National Defence Academy (NDA); it is located in Khadakwasla and provides army training. It is a joint training center for the Navy, Air Force, and Army. Through my nephew Puneet, I got to know many things about the rigorous army training. We visited the campus, which was spread across a hill with a lake on one side. The canteen there was also very famous for catering to a large number of students at the same time. Puneet used to visit on some weekends to enjoy homemade food. We had the pleasure of watching his passing out parade with his parents when he completed his final year. Later, his younger brother Sohit also passed out from NDA, and now Puneet's son, the next generation, has also trained there and joined the Indian Air Force.

Meanwhile, my elder daughter Manjari got pregnant, and I went to Haridwar for her delivery. She was blessed with a healthy baby boy through a cesarean section on the 20th of July 1991. It was painful for me to see my daughter go through the pain of a cesarean section, as all my children were born through normal delivery.

Being a grandparent and holding the child in my arms was such a new and beautiful feeling.

After that, we started visiting Haridwar regularly for Ayush's birthday, and Leena would also join us. The first time Manjari came to visit by flight, Ayush was only six months old and cried throughout the journey, making his mother run around from the cabin to the seat and vice versa. He was the first grandchild in our house and was pampered by everyone. I had already started making sweaters and different types of woollen caps as it was cold in Haridwar. Later, I also learned to make soft toys and created monkeys, dogs, and other animals for Ayush. With my newfound skill in making soft toys, I began teaching classes on how to make them during the day.

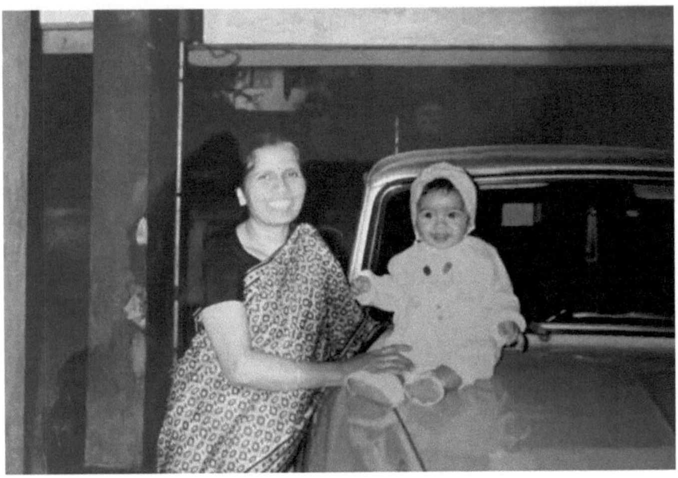

With Ayush on his first Pune visit

Meanwhile, Mintoo was excelling in his studies. He passed the N.T.S. exam with good marks and was felicitated at the Apte Sabha Grah in Maharashtra. Only a few students from his school were selected, and we felt immensely proud watching him receive recognition. In the meantime, Leena completed her M.B.B.S. and returned with a wealth of experience from medical college, which was new to our family as no one had previously pursued a career in medicine. She then completed a one-year internship and was fortunate to be selected for the D.C.H. program at Ruby Hall Clinic, one of Pune's prestigious hospitals. It was a residential course, and she had to work tirelessly day and night, gaining practical experience in dealing with infants and children. We often visited her with food as she was always busy with her patients, occasionally taking her to nearby hotels for a change of scene. She completed her D.C.H. and subsequently continued to work in the PICU at Ruby hall for few years.

Meanwhile, Chacha, who was quite old by then, fell ill and was bedridden for about five months. Sadly, on Makar Sankranti Day, January 14, 1994, he passed away. It was a tremendous loss for us, especially for my husband, as he was Chacha's only son. The loss of parents is something that can never be fully recovered.

However, life moves on. For some time, I would still hear Chacha calling my name, as he often did when he was sick, as I was the one who was always at home, although we had someone to look after him. My daughter Leena's marriage had already been arranged with a Saraswat Maharashtrian boy from Sahawas Society, and it was solemnized in May 1995. All my siblings and relatives attended the wedding.

Meanwhile, Mintoo had also taken his 12th-grade exams that year. We had booked a flat in Aundh in 1993, and the furniture work was underway. We planned to move after Leena's marriage, so we shifted in June 1995.

In Aundh, our building, Megha Terraces, was located in a very open area, with the only nearby colony being Wireless Colony. It was a newly developed area at that time, in a prime location. Aundh village was within walking distance, where the vegetable market and Hanuman temple were situated. We would visit the temple every Saturday. Nearby, there were also Aundh gymkhana, a park, and Parihar Chowk, which had a posh vegetable market and various shops for groceries, sweets, and clothes.

Mintoo's exam results were out, and his hard work had paid off. He passed with an excellent percentage and secured admission on merit to C.O.E.P., which was highly competitive. We purchased a motorcycle for him to commute to college. C.O.E.P. is one of the prestigious government engineering colleges established in 1854, and many celebrities have graduated from there. Leena opened her own clinic in Sahawas Society, where she resided with her in-laws.

In our new building society, all the flat owners were enthusiastic about their new homes. My friend, Mrs. Suguna Rao from Prabhat Road, had also moved in; she lived on the first floor while I lived on the second floor. As per the tradition in Maharashtra, we bought a Ganpati murti for the first time on Ganesh Chaturthi, and the entire society celebrated for ten days. Various competitions such as cooking, rangoli, fancy dress, and musical chairs were organized for children and adults. Cultural programs were also held, and the building kitty started as well.

I had some free time, so I started taking tuitions. Meanwhile, we decided to sell our Satna bungalow as it was challenging to manage it from our current location, and renting it out would require frequent visits.

My son Mintoo, who was studying in COEP, participated in the annual college function. The event was graced by Lila Poonawala, a famous industrialist, as the chief guest. COEP's annual social gathering was renowned for its spectacular regatta, where enthusiastic students competed in a series of boat races. It was a breathtaking event that required the hard work of many students, and it had been taking place for the past 80 years. The regatta took place on the Mulla River, where the boat club is located, and Mintoo was part of it. As a proud parent, I enjoyed the event immensely.

Meanwhile, in 1997, my husband, who was working in Z.F.India and enjoying his post as a General Manager, expressed his desire to start his own business. He may have been inspired by seeing some successful friends in business, as the grass is always greener on the other side. He purchased a plot in Chakan and entered into a partnership to set up a plant for P.P.(Polypropelene) straps. However, the venture was not as successful as planned. To support my husband, I also pursued a diploma in computer studies, and we purchased a computer.

PART 9

Life Has Its Ups And Downs

Today was my 60th birthday, July 4th 2003. We had a small get-together with family in the evening. Like all birthdays, we celebrated with great enthusiasm and homemade delicacies. Turning 60 is an important milestone, as well as the 75th birthday in most Indian households. It serves as a reminder that one is stepping into old age and a new era is beginning.

As age caught up with me, I started experiencing some minor health problems. Leena, my second daughter who is a doctor and our local guardian, introduced us to Dr. Renu Mahtani, M.D., a renowned practitioner near our house. Dr. Renu became our family doctor, and later on, she started yoga classes. I was among the first few students to join in 2005. The yoga classes have now grown into a large Param Yoga Institute. Yoga became an integral part of my life and has helped me immensely in coping with mental and physical problems. After a few years, my husband also joined the yoga classes.

Mintoo, my son in Bombay, was doing well in his career. He purchased his first car, a black Wagon R. Whenever we visit Bombay, he loved taking us around in his car to different places like Malabar Hill, Hanging Garden, Haji Ali Dargah, Juhu Beach, and Chaupati for sightseeing. He would show us the bungalows of various heroes like Amitabh Bachchan, Shahrukh Khan, Salman Khan, and others. Among those early visits to Bombay, there is one memorable experience that I still vividly remember.

Joggers Park was a place where we used to go in the morning for a walk and have some juice from the cart outside. We would then have breakfast at a place of our choice. Occasionally, we attended cultural programs in the evening at Joggers Park, such as classical music concerts and qawwali performances by the famous Sabri Brothers. Even now, whenever we visit Mumbai, we make it a point to go to Joggers Park, which has grown significantly and become a popular spot for Mumbaikars to unwind and enjoy the sea breeze in the evenings.

A memorable breakfast place was at South Indian restaurant near Ruia College, Mani's. They served amazing idli, dosa, vada, and filter coffee. The waiters provided efficient service, and the aroma of filter coffee filled the air. It was a small place but still very popular, and we had to go early in the morning to avoid long queues. South Indian breakfast was a favorite for our entire family, so it was a double pleasure for us.

We also frequented Rama Nayak, an old eating place near Matunga Railway Station. This small and clean place required us to purchase coupons before getting served with food on banana leaves. Eating with our hands was encouraged, and wasting food was not allowed, as indicated by a board. The owner, who stood and supervised the entire process, ensured a unique dining experience. However, the concept of queues was followed by most places in Mumbai.

Mintoo also took us to my house in Parel. It was where I spent my childhood and lived with my family in the Parel Railway Colony. It was nostalgic and brought back many old memories. Although it was not in good condition anymore, the colony still existed, evoking many memories.

We also went to Prithvi Theatre. Prithviraj Kapoor was a legendary actor, and his dream was Prithvi Theatre, which his son Shashi Kapoor and his wife Jennifer accomplished. Now, Shashi Kapoor's son Kunal and daughter Sanjana are taking care of it. The theater also has a nice café where we sat for a while and caught a glimpse of some theater actors.

Another eatery we visited was Swati Snacks, where, apart from enjoying tasty and mouth-watering Gujarati dishes, I had my favorite Kala Khatta ice gola, which I have loved since my school days. Others in the family enjoyed their favorite Malai Kulfi.

Another breakfast place was Govinda Restaurant in the ISKCON temple. The atmosphere there was very peaceful, and the food was incredibly tasty. They started by serving natural juice and herbal tea, followed by a variety of snacks made in pure ghee. From puri bhaji to sabudana khichadi, idli dosa, and various types of sweet dishes, the food was served with so much love and devotion. It is said that 56 varieties of sweets are offered to Lord Krishna as bhog. I can't forget the experience of enjoying such delicious food in such a serene environment.

These are the places I remember from my initial visits. I will share more later, as the list is unlimited. Now, let's turn to my elder daughter, Cuckoo. During my visits to her in Haridwar, where she lived with her joint family, I noticed that something was wrong in her marriage. She was teaching at Delhi Public School and tried her best to keep things normal, hiding the problems as much as possible. However, in any relationship, you cannot clap with one hand. As a result, she was emotionally wrecked inside, and even Ayush, my grandson, was suffering. Gradually, the truth became clear to us, and the situation deteriorated to the point where she decided to come to Pune with Ayush. We wholeheartedly supported her decision, as we couldn't bear to see them in such conditions. Ayush always stayed by his mommy's side, aware of the real situation.

With the help of friends , well-wishers and relatives, she finally came to Pune with Ayush in January 2006. Later, support came from unexpected sources. It wasn't easy and took some time to settle and accept the facts for all of us. But as the saying goes, "Sometimes life doesn't give you what you want, not because you don't deserve it, but because you deserve much more." This came true for Cuckoo. She is now in a very good position, and Ayush as well. It marked a new era in their lives and ours as well. Cuckoo joined yoga classes to overcome the emotional trauma, and Ayush joined various classes like karate, badminton, and yoga to keep him busy. Meanwhile, I was busy accompanying Ayush to all his classes, working to bring happiness back into his life and make it normal. My life also underwent significant changes. My cooking skills, which had been idle for some time, came back to life. Now that Ayush was at home, I prepared different dishes like pav bhaji, ragda pattice, and, with the new microwave, even pizzas for him. I loved making moong dal kachori and jhol for Mintoo when he would come home on weekends, not forgetting Leena, who also visited on some weekends.

In March, when the new school session began, Ayush joined D.A.V. School in the 9th grade. It is a highly reputed school near our house, where he studied until the 12th grade. He was also a sincere and intelligent boy, just like my other children. I believe I have always been blessed in the long run.

After trying for a few days, Cuckoo succeeded in getting a job at the IndSearch Institute on Law College Road. Her MBA degree from Pune University proved to be a plus point. As I mentioned earlier, hard work and sincerity paid off for her. We purchased a two-wheeler for her to commute to college. It is difficult to rely on public transportation in Pune as the bus service is not very reliable. In 2006, my husband also purchased a Tata Indica as his Maruti car had become very old, and he had to travel extensively for business purposes.

Slowly, things started to settle down by 2007. Time proved to be a great healer. In March, we made a family trip to Mahabaleshwar, a famous hill station. Though we had visited before, going as a complete family added a different level of enjoyment. The journey took around 3 to 4 hours, with a break at a famous Misal Pav (a popular Maharashtrian dish) outlet for breakfast,. We visited various points in Mahabaleshwar, including Venna Lake and Wilson Point, and explored Mapro Garden, where we enjoyed strawberries with cream amidst the beautiful strawberry gardens. It was a delightful trip, and we stocked up on jams, honey, jellies, sweets, and sherbets to bring back as souvenirs.

I have fond memories of Hotel Prospect in Panchgani, where we stayed during many of our visits. It was our favorite hotel, situated in a beautiful location with charming cottages and a swimming pool. An Irani family owns the place and are very hospitable. We would enjoy morning tea and biscuits brought to us on a kettle and tray while sitting on a swing. Nearby, we visited Table Land Point, Sydney Point, Mapro Garden, and the local market to purchase strawberries before heading back. The food at Hotel Prospect was delicious, catering to both vegetarian and non-vegetarian preferences.

These are just a few places I remember from our early visits, and the list could go on. Each place holds special memories and has contributed to our journey as a family.

Our next trip was to Goa. We had booked a resort near the beach, allowing us to enjoy the morning and evening at the seashore. The following day, we visited the famous Basilica of Jesus, which showcased impressive architecture and housed the mortal remains of St. Francis Xavier, a renowned saint. We also visited the famous Mangeshi Temple and indulged in delicious seafood, which our family loves. Refreshed and rejuvenated, we returned from our trip.

As we settled down, Ayush appeared for his 10th-grade exams, and during the holidays, we planned a visit to South India. We started with Bangalore, where we stayed at our friend Mr. Singh's place. He had started his own business and was now settled in Bangalore with a big bungalow. His son Sanjay had also joined him in the business. We enjoyed their hospitality and explored Bangalore, including its famous sights.

Next, we visited Mysore, where Sanjay, being a member of the golf club, arranged for us to stay in the golf club's guest house. We visited the renowned Mysore Palace and Chamundi Hill. We also visited Brindavan Gardens, located 12 km from the city, which offered a beautiful and colorful fountain show in the evening. The crowds had grown since my last visit when the movie "Jhanak Jhanak Payal Baje" was being shot there. Mysore silk sarees, sandal soap, and wooden showpieces are famous in the region, and we purchased a few showpieces and sarees.

From Mysore, we proceeded to Ooty, a famous hill station, where we stayed at the reputed Hotel Savoy, a grand heritage hotel. The hotel was located in the city but had its own beautiful campus. Apart from enjoying the natural beauty, we cherished the hospitality and delicious food at Savoy. It was a memorable trip.

My younger brother, Anoop, who was working at Bank of India, got transferred to Navi Mumbai. He and his family moved to a quarter in the Nerul, Bank of India colony near DY Patil Stadium. Whenever we traveled to Mumbai in our Indica car to visit Mintoo's house, we would sometimes take a break and have breakfast at Anoop's place before proceeding further.

During one of our trips to Mumbai, when we visited Mintoo's cabin in Bandra Kurla Complex, we saw many awards he had received. We felt proud as parents. As usual, Mintoo took us to different restaurants for lunch and dinner, including some of the finest Chinese restaurants in Mumbai, which I enjoyed. In the evenings, he would often take us to his favorite place, Taj Mahal Tea House. We gradually learned to enjoy these experiences, realizing that it was his hard-earned money and a way for him to spend quality time with us. Although I still had the habit of occasionally expressing my concerns about spending too much money at these restaurants, I felt happy as a parent. Some of his restaurant choices were Pali Bhavan, Soda Bottle Openerwala, Masala Library, and Mocha's for desert, each offered a unique dining experience.

I have a habit of finding a library wherever I stay because I love reading. Mintoo also developed a love for books and reading. When he was young, we used to visit bookstores on MG Road, East Street, or Deccan in Pune. If he found a bookstore or books for sale, he would spend hours there. His love for books continues, although he has less time for reading due to his busy career. Besides books, I also enjoy reading magazines as they keep me in touch with current people and situations.

During my search for a library, I came across a wonderful one in Aundh called Just Books. They had a great variety of books, especially many Hindi books by famous authors that I hadn't found elsewhere in Maharashtra. I started reading the autobiography of Harivansh Rai Bachchan, which was in four volumes and incredibly honest. I also read books by authors like Manu Bhandari, Bhagwati Charan Varma, Mahasweta

Devi, Rabindranath Tagore, Sarat Chandra, Vrindavan Lal Verma, and many more. The list is endless. The best part about Just Books was that they had a chain, so even when I visited Leena's place in Kothrud, I could exchange books at Just Books, which I loved.

Meanwhile, our yoga classes, which started with just a few members, was rapidly growing into an institution. Initially, Dr. Renu used to invite all her yoga members to her house for snacks during Diwali, but now we were celebrating an annual day with cultural activities in a hall. After a few years, my husband also joined the yoga classes, and we became active members in cultural programs and picnics. Our group of 20 developed a strong bond that continued throughout the years, and now we have a WhatsApp group and attend online classes due to the pandemic.

Our friends from Nasik, Mr. Rajgopal and Jayshree, invited us to their son's marriage in Kerala, which was to be performed at the Guruvayur Temple. They were Malayalees whom we had also visited in Pune when we went to the Ayyappa Temple in Nigdi on 2-3 occasions. Jayshree, being very orthodox and traditional, had vowed to perform her son's marriage at the Guruvayur Temple. This gave us an opportunity to visit Kerala, and Mintoo planned for the three of us to go together.

So, we flew from Mumbai to Kochi and then drove to the Guruvayur Temple. We stayed at Hotel Bansuri, which was located near the temple and had made arrangements for our stay. Guruvayurappan, the deity worshipped at the temple, is said to be an incarnation of Lord Vishnu. The wedding took place early in the morning at the temple, and we got ready to attend. The temple was within walking distance, and it was a very big temple with beautiful architecture. The temple had three mandaps, raised platforms in front of the temples. All the close friends, relatives, and parents of the bride and groom, with big garlands, stood in a queue. The time for each marriage was already fixed, and everyone was quite punctual. When Nitin's and the girl's names were announced on the microphone, they went on stage with their parents, exchanged garlands, and the boy tied the mangal sutra around the girl's neck. Within 15 minutes, the marriage was over. We, along with all the relatives, stood at a distance and witnessed the shortest marriage we had ever seen. We came to know that 300 marriages take place daily at the temple. After the wedding, we went to a nearby hall that Rajgopal had booked for a reception. The groom was dressed in a white kurta with a zari border and mundu (lungi), while the bride wore a heavy white zari saree and lots of jewellery. They were seated on a stage with big, thick, colorful garlands. We wished them on the stage to bless them and then had a simple lunch served on banana leaves. It included rice, sambar, avial, rasam, papad, and many varieties of chutney and pickles. Coconut was mostly used in all their dishes. After that, we were served a sweet dish called payasam, which is a rice kheer but prepared differently from what we are used to.

After the marriage and lunch, we decided to visit the temple for darshan and stood in a long queue. Before that, my husband and Mintoo purchased mundu for themselves, which were compulsory for entering the temple. After a long wait, we had darshan of the black, huge murti (idol) with four arms. The temple had beautiful architecture, and many diyas were lit. On occasions like Janmashtami, the entire temple is lit up with diyas, and it must look beautiful. Ayyappa, whom they worship, is actually a young Krishna.

We stayed overnight and the next morning started our drive from Kochi to Munnar, which took about 12 hours. In Munnar, we stayed at Windermere Estate, a huge and beautiful resort with a view of nature, mountains, and tea and coffee plantations. The surroundings were lush green, offering a lovely view. The hotel had spacious rooms decorated with traditional, huge beds and furnishings. The food was also good, with both Indian and Continental options available. They even offered us a small trekking experience. After spending a day there, we proceeded to Thekkady, our next destination, enjoying the clouds, birds, and mountain streams along the way.

In Thekkady, we stayed in a cottage owned by a forest officer, who entertained us with good food and many stories from his working days. We also went for a small trek, visited a cardamom plantation, explored the spice market, and even visited a tea museum to learn about tea processing at different stages. We also had a short visit to Alleppey, which is known for its plantations. After enjoying our stay in the lovely cottage, we proceeded to Kumarakom.

In Kumarakom, we had booked us a stay at the Taj, a wonderful lake resort. As soon as we reached, we were welcomed with garlands and coconut water, which we loved after the drive. While waiting for our room, we had a glance at the beautiful surroundings. What a lovely place!

At the Taj, we had a 2-day and 3-night stay with good surroundings and spacious rooms. In the evening, the resort was lit with earthen diyas, giving the lake a gracious look. Our room had a lovely view of ducks and cranes in the lake, enjoying their food. Apart from enjoying the fishing and cycling in the resort, we also had dinner accompanied by traditional cultural dances. It was a lovely holiday with good food.

Next, we went for a backwater drive in a cruise. In the houseboat, we had a wonderful time. As soon as we boarded, they brought fresh fish and prepared a delicious lunch of fish and rice sambhar. While returning, we enjoyed the sunset as well. It was a truly memorable lunch, and we had such a lovely time.

After that, we got back to our routine. In between, we took some trips to Bombay, and then Mintoo, my husband and I went to Matheran in November. My husband took his Tata Indica, as usual. We had booked a room at Verandah in the Forest, a good heritage hotel in a British-era mansion. It was close to Lake Charlotte. We visited many points like Echo Point and Lord Point, enjoying the natural beauty and good food. There is a toy train running between Neral and Matheran, which was a nostalgic experience for me as I remembered my childhood visits with my parents. However, it was quite crowded now, with ponies running between the railway tracks. The red soil all around added to the charm. We enjoyed the trip, but while coming back in the car, we had many leeches in the tires that accompanied us to our house, and removing them was painful.

Meanwhile, my second daughter Leena, who was a child specialist and doing quite well with her own practice, was not satisfied and wanted to do something concerning developmental pediatrics. In 2008, she had done a distance education course in developmental neurology from Kerala when the concept was very new and very few colleges in India offered such courses. In 2008 itself she got an opportunity to join Bharatiya Vidyapeeth, one of the renowned institutions, starting a unit in developmental pediatrics. She also furthered her education and over time the developmental unit and its popularity grew with her as the Incharge. This change proved to be lucky for her, and she made a good name for herself while also making some good friends, including Dr. Kalrao, who became her mentor. We are very proud of the work she is doing.

Meanwhile, my son, Mintoo, was also progressing in his career at ICICI and his vehicle also changed from a Wagon R to a Honda City, but he was still attached to his first car which was handed over to Leena, who needed it to commute to college, as her home was far away. It seemed that in our family, men were too attached to their vehicles, and my husband was the leader in that aspect. Every weekend was dedicated to cleaning and washing his vehicle, regardless of what type of car it was.

In the meantime, my grandson, Ayush, also appeared for his 12th-grade exams. The family needed a break, so the children planned a visit to Udaipur and Mount Abu in 2011. We first went to Bombay to Mintoo's house and then took a flight from Bombay to Ahmedabad. From there, we traveled by Innova car to Udaipur, enjoying the nice roads of Ahmedabad. In Udaipur, we stayed at Hotel Sheraton, a lovely heritage hotel with a great location, overlooking Lake Pichola on one side and the Aravalli hills on the other. Udaipur is known as the city of lakes, and the hotel and its surroundings looked amazing at night. The next day, we visited Chittorgarh Fort, a world heritage site. The fort was huge and had a rich history of Mewar. It had wonderful architecture and was well-maintained with museums, galleries, paintings, armory, and big chambers with intricate wood carvings. Next to it, there was a vintage car museum where the men were busy enjoying the collection of vintage cars, while we ladies sat together and chatted. On our way back, we enjoyed the Rajasthani dish of dal bati churma at a local eatery and witnessed a beautiful sunset. Our stay in Udaipur was comfortable with delicious food and spacious rooms.

The next day, we proceeded to Mount Abu in our Innova, enjoying the sight of men in colorful pagadis and ladies in colorful ghagra cholis all around. On our way, we had a traditional Rajasthani breakfast of phaphra and jalebis, and we also had a view of Nakki Lake. We reached a cottage that was booked for our stay in Mount Abu.

The next day, we went to Rock View Point and did a bit of trekking.. While some people climbed higher points, we simply sat and enjoyed the view. We visited more temples and eventually reached Mount Shikha, the highest peak of the Aravalli range. There, we found a beautiful temple dedicated to Dattatreya. We had previously seen many Datta temples in Maharashtra, but this one was special. Outside the temple, there were many stalls selling marble items, mostly khalbatta and hursa used for making chapattis. We also purchased two of them but later realized they were too heavy to carry on the flight. We also bought some wind chimes as souvenirs for our friends.

Our next visit was to the famous Brahma Kumari Ashram in Shantivan. We had heard so much about it, as many of our friends are followers and visit the ashram once a year. It was a very nice and peaceful place with meditation halls. It was a good experience for us.

Back at the cottage, no trip is complete for my daughters without some shopping. They bought some bandhini dresses and colorful bedsheets. This way, one more trip came to an end, and we returned to our routine.

Upon our return, Ayush's exam results came out, and he passed with flying colors. He got admission to Sinhagad College of Engineering to pursue a Bachelor's degree in Mechanical Engineering, which was his preferred branch. We purchased a motorcycle for him as it was essential for commuting to college, and his career path began to take shape.

Meanwhile, as our children insisted, my husband decided to wind up his business and sell his factory. They wanted him to lead a retired life, which was initially difficult for him as he was a workaholic. However, he gradually adjusted and made friends in the park. He also joined a senior citizens association to keep himself busy.

I found myself busier now with reading books since a new library called Meridian had opened near our house. They even provided home delivery and had a great collection of English books. In the evenings, I started spending an hour there, enjoying various magazines, while my husband walked in the park and joined a group of friends.

We continued our yoga classes, which kept us busy. It was during these classes that I got the opportunity to read books by many English authors, such as Shobha De, Anuja Chauhan, Khushwant Singh, Daniel Steel, Anita Desai, Nayantara Sehgal, Preeti Shenoy, Ruskin Bond, and the list is endless. There's a treasure trove of books, and although I have read around 200, I want to read more. So many new young authors are emerging with new ideas, and it's a pleasure for me to spend time with books. Nowadays, libraries are being replaced by tablets, iPads, and Kindles. I also read books on my Kindle now, reminiscing about the old times.

Life was moving on, and everyone was busy. Mintoo had formed a group of close friends, including Binaifer, Shridhar, Anindya, Nisha, and Sri. Whenever we were in Bombay, they would meet us. They had become like family to Mintoo. Leena and Cuckoo were also doing well, and Ayush was busy with college.

PART 10

Travel & Food

Travel has been an integral part of my life. My father was fond of traveling, being in the Railways, and he never wasted his first-class passes. After marriage, my husband developed a liking for travel as well, and we traveled extensively, and now my son, Mintoo, follows in their footsteps. The difference lies in our travel experiences. With my father, we mostly traveled by train to religious places, staying in railway retiring rooms, relatives' places, or sometimes dharamshalas. With my husband's L.T.A benefits, we started staying in good hotels, enjoying diverse cuisine while traveling to different states.

Now, with my son, things have changed for the better. He not only enjoys visiting new places and relishing different types of food but also values traveling with family, especially his parents and siblings. This is a rare quality. Both my daughters also share a love for travel, and together, we have explored various places and savored local delicacies. Initially, I used to feel concerned about the expenses incurred on hotels and food, but over time, I began to relish and appreciate these experiences.

In 2014, my grandson Ayush completed his engineering and expressed his desire to pursue an M.S. in the U.S. To prepare for it while working, our children planned a visit to Singapore. It would provide Ayush with valuable exposure and serve as a refreshing break for the entire family. It was my first foreign trip, and the excitement we felt as a whole family made it truly unforgettable.

My children love to plan their own trips instead of relying on travel agents. They take charge of flight bookings, and from the moment they start planning, the excitement begins for them. They carefully select accommodations that suit our preferences, providing comfort for us as senior citizens and also fitting our budget. Since our family is composed of food enthusiasts, they also create a shortlist of restaurants based on ratings. They coordinate among themselves, taking care of everything while we simply enjoy the process.

For our trip to Singapore from Bombay, we boarded a flight to Kuala Lumpur where we had breakfast. From there, we proceeded to Changi Airport and took a taxi to our destination, the IBIS hotel. The hotel is situated amidst impressive skyscrapers and boasts a wonderful location, conveniently close to a bus stop. Traveling in Singapore deserves accolades. They have made it easy by issuing a card at the airport, which can be used for buses, trams, and the Metro. Throughout our trip, we extensively used the Metro and I particularly enjoyed the announcements made inside. I still remember one particular sentence: "Next station, Dhobi Ghat. Doors are closing." The discipline and strict adherence to rules by everyone were truly admirable. Singapore is a colorful city offering a wide variety of food options.

During our stay, we visited various attractions such as Sentosa Island Resort, the shopping mall Aquarium with its abundance of big fishes, whales, and impressive reptiles. One of my personal highlights was the Jurong Bird Park, where I encountered numerous friendly and colorful birds, especially parrots. We also explored Buddha temples, Riverside Point, and the zoo, where we saw many animals, including large chimpanzees. We had the chance to witness a laser show, a water rain dance, and a captivating dolphin show where dolphins displayed their playful tricks. I can't forget to mention Clarke Quay, as the Singapore River flows through the heart of this vibrant area.

Aside from sightseeing, my family, who are passionate about food, indulged in various eating joints of their choice. Mintoo, especially, was delighted with the wide variety of sushi available, as he has a fondness for it.

We also dined at a famous restaurant called Fatty's, where everyone, except me, enjoyed crab and other delicious fish delicacies. As a vegetarian, I had to contend myself with mushrooms and potatoes. However, we found a solution at a South Indian restaurant near our hotel, which served delightful sambar rice with papad. Additionally, we explored Little India, a place that provides glimpses of India along with delicious Indian cuisine.

Of course, we couldn't leave without indulging in some shopping, particularly at IKEA. At that time, IKEA was a novelty, but it has since opened many stores in India as well. The children went on a shopping spree and bought numerous bags filled with useful items that have lasted us a long time.

And just like that, our first foreign trip concluded on a happy note, leaving us with cherished memories.

After returning, Ayush joined Z.F. India Company while simultaneously preparing for his Master's degree. Finally, he received admission to Michigan Technological University. We were overjoyed as his ambition was about to be fulfilled. His mother, my daughter Cuckoo, started training him in cooking, washing utensils, and other household chores, as he would have to do everything by himself due to being a student with a limited budget.

On August 15, 2015, he left for the U.S., and we were all filled with a mixture of happiness and anxiety. It was his first time traveling alone to a foreign country at such a young age. We went to see him off at the Bombay airport. Thus began a new chapter in his life.

In September 2016, it was my husband's 75th birthday, and Mintoo called us to Bombay to celebrate. The next day, he took us in his Honda City to Marine Drive and then to the Trident Hotel on Nariman Point, where he had made a two-day reservation. On our way, we passed by the Racecourse, where we had a delightful continental lunch at Gallops with Mintoo's close friends. The view of the racecourse was splendid. Later, we proceeded to the hotel, where he had booked spacious rooms on the 21st floor with a breathtaking view of the sea. It felt as if we were on a cruise ship, and I spent most of my time sitting in front of the window, enjoying the crowd at Marine Drive and the vastness of the sea. We relished a delicious brunch with a wide variety of dishes, along with the hospitality of the five-star hotel. After a refreshing two-day stay, we returned home.

In 2016, Mintoo planned a trip to Sikkim, Darjeeling, and Calcutta. We flew from Bombay to Calcutta and then took a flight to Bagdogra Airport, followed by a taxi to Siliguri. In Siliguri, we were welcomed as guests at the home of Mintoo's college friend Rahul Lakhotia and his parents. Rahul belongs to a renowned family in Siliguri, with substantial ancestral property. We had a comfortable night's stay and dinner with Rahul's parents, his wife, and children. The next morning, we proceeded to Gangtok, our next destination.

During our stay, we chose the Tashi Dalek Hotel, which belonged to Rahul's family. It was one of the best hotels with a lovely view from its terrace. We selected a table that offered a picturesque view and savored delicious food. It was there that we had the pleasure of meeting Rahul's 80-year-old grandfather, who was dressed smartly in a white shirt and jacket. He was a regular entertainer, sharing his adventurous and interesting anecdotes about starting his business at a young age and traveling to China on a yak for business purposes. His enthusiasm and interesting stories made a lasting impression on us, despite his age.

The following morning, we visited the Nathula Checkpost in a jeep provided by the hotel. Thanks to the VIP pass, we could drive till the last point, which meant we had to walk only a short distance. Otherwise, the journey would have been challenging with numerous steps and sub-zero temperatures. Due to the VIP pass, we were ushered into an air-conditioned hall where we were served coffee by a local official. The Nathula Checkpost marks the border between China and India, with a sturdy fence dividing the two countries. We waved to each other enthusiastically, with the Indians displaying even more excitement.

The beauty of the snow-covered Nathula Mountain Pass is indescribable; words fall short in capturing its magnificence. However, as we descended, the cold and hunger started to set in. We stumbled upon a dhaba where we relished Thukpa, their traditional dish, served in a large bowl—a hot noodle soup with chicken and momos. The flavors were comforting and delicious.

After two delightful days exploring Chang and other points of interest, we proceeded to Pelling. The road conditions were challenging, adding an adventurous touch to our journey. At one point,we saw a wagon R stuck on the road, and all the drivers promptly stepped out to lend a helping hand. Eventually, we reached our hotel, where we were greeted with a lovely view.

In Pelling, we visited the Kanchenjunga Falls, Rumtek Monastery, Rumtek Monastery (also known as Dharma Chakra Centre), Pegmyantse monastery, Rabdentse ruins and many other ancient monasteries. It was a marvelous experience to explore these serene places amidst such tranquility. Another highlight was the Singshore Suspension Bridge, as well as witnessing both sunrise and sunset at Tiger Hill and the helipad. Waiting at the helipad, we marveled at nature's splendor—a breathtaking view that defies description. Sikkim, with its simplicity, warm-hearted people, and untouched natural beauty, left a lasting impression.

From there, we took a taxi to Darjeeling, the "Queen of Hills," where we had reservations at the Cedar Inn Hotel—a charming place. During our stay, we visited the Japan Temple, Peace Pagoda, and St. Paul School, which had been a shooting location for the Hindi film

"Main Hoon Na." We also had the opportunity to visit Happy Valley, where we witnessed the tea-making process. In the hotel, we were delighted by the traditional attire of the waiters, donning red pagdis, as they served us tea and breakfast with utmost love and care. We indulged in numerous cups of tea and savored the diverse cuisines of the region, thoroughly enjoying every moment.

Next on our itinerary was the Toy Train, a century-old heritage of the Himalayan Railways. Traveling in the steam engine amidst the enchanting landscape was a nostalgic experience, especially when we stopped at Ghum Station, which housed a museum showcasing the history of locomotive engines through a captivating photo gallery. As my father had worked in the railways, it held a special emotional connection, evoking memories of him. It was even more enjoyable as we reminisced about old Hindi movies where trains often played a significant role, with roads running parallel to the train tracks.

Afterward, we visited the Tibet market, Chamba Lake, Rock Garden, Garam Sadak, Mall Road, and then went to Bade Bazar for shopping. We purchased sweaters and shawls for my daughters since they were not with us on the trip.

Next, we proceeded to our next destination, Kolkata, where we stayed at the Golden Park Hotel near Park Street, a central location. We visited the Victoria Memorial, Belur Math, Tagore House, Howrah Bridge on the Hooghly River, the Rabindranath Museum, Charausta Market, St. John's Church, and more. Of course, a trip to Kolkata wouldn't be complete without visiting Kali Ghat and the Kali Temple. A pandit there insisted on performing a special puja for us. We had the opportunity to behold the grand murti (idol) of Kali Maa before returning.

Now, let me share the list of eateries we visited. Trinka's Hotel, where a famous song from the movie "Parineeta" was filmed for dinner, Peter Cat Restaurant, Flurry's Bakery, and the famous Kewpies Thali for lunch—each dining experience was unique. And we couldn't resist trying the street food like churmura, ghughni chaat, puchka, and various Bengali sweets like luchi aloo dum. We savored every delicious bite.

Our next agenda was exploring the leather market and purchasing purses for everyone from Sreeleathers. We found a great variety of high-quality leather purses, and we bought many of them, some of which I still have. The trip came to an end there.

On March 11th, 2017, during the Holi festival, Mintoo had a four-day holiday, and we didn't want to waste it. So, a trip to Dubai was planned. Dubai is one of the most popular and modern cities in the world, just a short flight from Mumbai. It's a perfect destination for relaxation with its white sandy beaches, and the Dubai Mall is the largest mall in the world. Some ladies of kitty group often go to Dubai for shopping, but personally, I was least interested in shopping. We stayed at the

Crowne Plaza Hotel and explored the city by metro and boat, visiting Deira Old Dubai, which has a remarkable gold market, and the Masala Market. Dubai is known for its pure gold. We also visited Jumeirah Beach, the Water Canal Bug Mall, and took a two-hour ferry tour. Mintoo's three friends joined us on some outings, providing great company. A visit to the famous Burj Khalifa, the highest observatory destination, offered a beautiful 360-degree view of the city. We enjoyed our time there and returned to our home in Mumbai.

My youngest brother, Anoop, along with his wife, Reeta, and their son Cheenu, had been residing in Wagholi for the past few years. We used to meet very often. On our next trip to Thailand, they decided to join us, making the trip even more enjoyable. We flew from Mumbai to Bangkok and stayed at the Citrus Hotel. We admired the beautiful Suvarnabhumi Airport before heading to the Hua Hin Beach resort. We traveled in the famous Tuk-tuk, a type of rickshaw, and even enjoyed the rain during our journeys. We went boating and visited various temples dedicated to Buddha, relishing the peaceful atmosphere and admiring the various forms and postures of Buddha sculpted in marble and gold. Needless to say, we indulged in delicious Thai street food, including fresh cut fruits and papaya salad, which was made instantly in a khalbatta with flavorful spices. After returning to the hotel, we also savored Thai green curry rice. It was a memorable trip, and while traveling in an SUV car, we played antakshari, making the journey even more unforgettable.

Meanwhile, on the home front, Ayush completed his MS degree and also secured a job in Kokomo, Indiana. Time flew by, and in December 2018, he returned for the visa renewal. As he arrived, we had a delightful family get-together planned, and we also decided to visit Goa. During our time in Goa, we explored Candolim Beach and other beautiful beaches, fully enjoying the sea and taking baths to relax. Each morning, we indulged in wonderful traditional Goan breakfast at various places, had a fabulous lunch at the Classic Ritz Hotel, and enjoyed dinner with drinks and dancing at the Kala More Hotel. We also made sure to visit the churches in Goa. Before we knew it, the trip came to an end, and after a few days, Ayush had to return to Kokomo.

A few days later, in July, it was my birthday, and the children planned a trip to Europe. We visited four countries: Amsterdam in the Netherlands, Paris in France, Lucerne in Switzerland, and Munich in Germany. It was an exciting trip, and I felt a mix of excitement and nervousness. I never thought I would have the opportunity to visit these places. On July 19, 2018, we departed from Mumbai on a Swiss Airways flight to Zurich, and then continued our journey to Amsterdam.

The immigration process at Zurich was a new experience for me, and I felt quite anxious as it was my first international trip. In Amsterdam, the children had chosen a beautiful place to stay, equipped with a well-equipped kitchen and all necessary facilities. My daughter Leena, who is a doctor, had a friend named Nienke who was from the Netherlands. Nienke joined us immediately and was of great help and excellent company during our stay in Amsterdam. Being a local, she not only assisted us in sightseeing and selecting local food recommendations, but she also cooked delicious pancakes for us. It was a wonderful experience.

We visited a fishing village and a shoe-making factory, where we saw big wooden shoes. One important aspect of Amsterdam was the disciplined cycling culture, and both Leena and Mintoo had a pleasant experience cycling there. We also discovered a variety of cheeses, similar to how in India we have large lumps of khoya (milk solid), there they had a wide range of cheese varieties. We bought some recommended cheeses suggested by Leena's friend, Nienke.

From Amsterdam, we traveled to Paris by the fastest train, Thalys. We stayed in a beautiful house and visited the famous Louvre Museum, where we admired art pieces like the Mona Lisa and the Sainte-Chapelle. We enjoyed street music, explored the Shakespeare Bookstore and Library, and went on a cruise. We also visited the Eiffel Tower, spending time taking photographs from different angles, and explored the Van Gogh Museum and various churches.

Our next destination was the dreamlike Lucerne in Switzerland. As usual, the children chose a lovely place to stay, within walking distance of the lake. We made it a point to visit the lake every evening to sit and enjoy its beauty.

Another plus point was Mili and John, my brother's daughter, with their cute child Sia, who joined us in Lucerne. They were great company as we went to the high peaks of the alps, took a cable car, went to Mount Titlis, and enjoyed snow, especially with Sia, who was, I think, 4 years old. Afterwards, we went on a cruise on lake Lucerne too.

Then we came to our final destination, Munich, Germany. Here we visited the Marienplatz, local markets and some other places of interest. I heard there are many gardens, and later I came to know they are beer gardens with beer and music. It was difficult for me to sit due to the smell of beer and meat, so children had to choose an open space where I ate lots of potatoes in different forms, but it was an enjoyable trip.

We came back to reality again, as we were back in Bombay.

As usual, after staying for some time at Mintoo's House, I came back to Pune.

And then, in April 2019, another trip to Dalhousie, Dharamshala & Amritsar was planned. Since many days my whole family wanted to visit the gurudwara at Amritsar, so the visit was a wish fulfilment. First by flight we went to Amritsar and from there in an Innova which was already booked we went to Dalhousie stayed in Grand View Hotel. From there we went to Khajjiar where we enjoyed some great natural beauty with mountain sheep, wild rabbits and some snow. In Dalhousie, I remember some wonderful architecture of British times and lovely churches. I think we took a road called garam sadak and there was a cute café where we had tasty Momos and Chinese food!

Then we proceeded to Dharamshala, which is home to the Dalai Lama and is supposed to be a centre for studying Buddhism. There was Kotwali Bazar full of woolen clothes. We went to McLeodgang Ganj to visit Namgyal monastery and the Dalai Lama Temple. Then based on recommendations from Leena's friends, we went to Norbulingka institute of Buddhist studies. There was such a peaceful and full atmosphere to unwind in the monastery, with a Buddha temple everywhere and fluttering prayer flags. I saw many monks in saffron robes. And for the famous prayer chanting, which is peaceful to the mind. We brought back some prayer flags for our home as well.

From there, we proceeded to Amritsar, our final destination of the trip. Here we stayed in the Ramada Hotel, a beautiful hotel near the Gurudwara. From there, the first thing we visited was, of course, Gurudwara, where we had a wonderful experience of darshan and enjoyed sitting on campus having kada prasad. Then in the restaurant, we had chole kulcha and lassi.

The next day we visited Jallianwala Bagh, which needs no introduction, and one museum too, in which only Mintoo was interested. I spent some time reading the history of the place.

Then the next day we went to Wagah Border, where my nephew, being in the army, could get us passes for watching the ceremony, which takes place every evening. It was a unique experience to see the big gates on both sides of India and Pakistan, the flags of both countries flying in the air, the march by Indian soldiers and the ceremony which takes place, which cannot be described but only enjoyed. A feeling of patriotism filled everyone as they shout loudly, "Bharat mata ki jai," and patriotic songs are put on speakers during the ceremony.

How can the trip be completed without shopping for some phulkari dress material which was bought in abundance by my daughters!

As Diwali approached, we decided to celebrate the festival in Coorg and Bekal. On October 25, 2019, we flew from Pune to Mangalore. After having a hearty breakfast at an ID restaurant in Mangalore, we proceeded to Coorg by car. The journey took around 5 hours.

In Coorg, we opted for a homestay to have a more authentic experience. The homestay was managed by a mother and son, who provided us with a traditional setting and amenities like hot water from a sigdi (traditional stove). In the evening, a fireplace was lit in one of the rooms. We enjoyed a variety of traditional dishes made from rice, bananas, and coconut, including fish and pork, which were favorites of my husband and children.

The next day, we visited a coffee plantation and saw other spice trees like cardamom, cloves, and peppercorns. We witnessed the process of sorting, blending, and roasting coffee beans, which gave us the delightful aroma of filter coffee. Tall silver oak and rosewood trees provided shelter to the coffee shrubs.

After our time in Coorg, we proceeded to Bekal Beach. We had booked a stay at Taj Bekal to celebrate Diwali. In the evening, we all dressed up for the festival of lights. The next day, we visited Bekal Fort and enjoyed the natural beauty of the sea.

From 2010 to 2019, we had many trips within India as well as abroad, and each one provided us with wonderful experiences. As the year 2019 came to an end, we celebrated the joyous occasion of December 31st. The next morning, it was the beginning of a new year, 2020.

PART 11

To New Beginnings

It was the year 2020, and my younger daughter was turning 50 years old. Time flies so quickly. When she was young, she loved birthday parties, and this year was especially significant for all of us. On January 28th, we planned a party, which was attended by some close relatives at the Novotel Hotel on Nagar Road. It was also my nephew Monu's 40th birthday, so the party was a family celebration.

Then, on March 10th, we celebrated the vibrant festival of Holi in Pune. Although it was celebrated in a simple traditional manner, we had a delicious lunch with mutton and gujia (a sweet associated with Holi). Little did we know that we would not meet for a long time after that.

News about the coronavirus and COVID-19 started to spread, but initially, we did not take it seriously.

However, as cases increased rapidly, a lockdown was declared on March 24th, 2020. For the first time, an atmosphere of fear and anxiety filled everyone's minds. Schools, colleges, and offices closed down, and maids stopped coming. Everyone had to do their own work, and online platforms became essential for reading, watching movies and shows, and shopping. The work from home culture became prevalent, and even our yoga classes moved online. We rearranged our furniture to create space for walking at home, as morning and evening walks outside were no longer possible.

Video calls became a lifeline for staying connected with loved ones. My daughter Leena, who is a doctor and lives in Kothrud, was busy like all doctors and couldn't visit us for six months. My son in Mumbai, who used to visit frequently, could only be seen through video calls. Fortunately, my daughter Manjari, who was technology savvy, was staying with us. As senior citizens, our children took great care of us, and we learned to play online games like Ludo to spend time together. I was even gifted adult drawing books to engage in a creative hobby. The frequent video calls with children and grandson brought our family even closer.

The lockdown and the COVID-19 pandemic have been extensively written about, so I will stop here. It was a challenging time for everyone, but it also brought out the resilience and creativity in people. Many small-scale businesses suffered, but new talents emerged, and online platforms saw a surge in popularity. It emphasized that everyone is capable of doing their own work and adapting to new circumstances.

.

Time continued to pass, and my birthday came around every year. Usually, an outing was planned for my birthday, but this year we had to be satisfied with video calls. A few days before my birthday, Mintoo suggested that I should write since I had read so much. The idea stuck in my mind, and I decided to pen down my autobiography.

I remembered that during my college days, I had written and even won a prize for my poem in the college magazine. Through the years, I had written many short stories, but I never sent them anywhere and eventually tore them up. I started writing, and it was worth giving it a try. I already had a tablet, so I asked Cuckoo to set it up for writing. In the month of my birthday, I began writing, considering it as a gift for my children.

As time passed, the number of COVID-19 cases started to decrease, and the vaccination campaign began. People started getting vaccinated, and their confidence started to return. The use of masks, sanitizers, and cleanliness became common, and people gradually started moving out of their homes. For us as well, our first outing after the lockdown was with Leena to Bhartiya Vidyapeeth for vaccination. It was a wonderful ride in the fresh air, passing by Dagdu Sheth Temple. It felt so good to be out in the open after so many days. Life started moving forward for us, and our first outing was to a bungalow in Khandala. AirBnB provided cooking and housekeeping services in some nice bungalows there. We celebrated my husband's 80th birthday with dance, music, and games.

As time passed, things started to return to normal. We began planning our trips again. We resumed our travels and visited Rajasthan, Kerala, Nasik, Sula Wines, and many other places. We met relatives and friends with great enthusiasm.

I feel it's time to finish my book now. I think I have lived through one more era, experiencing so many different periods since 1943. It feels good to have written something for my grandchildren so they can learn about our old times. Nowadays, with nuclear families and busy parents, children often lack the time to know about their family history. Everyone is caught up in the race of life. Undoubtedly, many achievements have been made, and each person has evolved as an individual, especially during the lockdown.

Women have undoubtedly become much stronger now and have come a long way since our times. I, too, have come a long way from my humble beginnings in Jhansi, where I spent my childhood, embarking on a beautiful and transformative journey.

I have often been a disciplinarian, pushing my children to be the best in everything. In later years, I may have become hyper and overly critical, but my husband and children have shown immense patience and understanding towards me.

To my children and grandchild, I want to express how fortunate I am to have them in my life, and I love them deeply from the core of my being. Being critical is simply a part of my nature.

I began writing my autobiography in July 2020 and now bring it to a close in 2023. So much has happened in the past three years. Manjari has completed her Ph.D., and my grandson Ayush, who is flourishing in the United States, paid us a long-awaited visit after four years. We had a fantastic time together, and I hope for many more joyful moments in the future.

Embracing a positive outlook on life has been instrumental for me, even though like everyone else, I have my moments of feeling low. For everyone reading this, I would like to impart the advice of staying positive and cherishing the joys that life offers.

I enjoyed my journey through my memories, hope you also enjoy reading it.

Acknowledgements

In the end, I would like to acknowledge all the people who helped me in writing this, especially my children Cuckoo, Leena and Mintoo, for encouraging me. I am grateful to my husband for always being there for me and for frequently changing jobs, which exposed us to various places and people.

When the lockdown started, Mintoo suggested that I read many books and encouraged me to write my own. It reminded me of my yoga friend, Shaila Kagal, who had written her memoirs dedicated to her father. I was one of the few readers who had the opportunity to read her manuscript, and I liked it. Last year, I got a tablet for reading, and downloaded Kindle and Magzster for reading magazines. Cuckoo made some settings for writing, and I began penning down my memories. As I started writing, it was an eye-opener, and all the memories started pouring in. I felt a sense of lightness and joy after writing.

I would like to express my gratitude to my elder brother, Sushil, whom we affectionately called Bade Bhaiya, and my younger sister, Usha, who helped me in recalling my younger days. We chatted and relished living those moments again, and it was a lot of fun.

I would like to thank my husband and children for everything, all my family, siblings, relatives, and friends for being a part of my life. Special thanks to Dr. Renu Mahtani, our family doctor and yoga teacher, who introduced me to yoga when I became a senior citizen and faced numerous health problems. Yoga has played a significant role in my life, as fitness is an essential aspect.

Thank you to everyone who has come into my life, as each person has taught me something valuable. Life is a great teacher, and it's important to keep our eyes open and never give up. I have been impatient with my children on many occasions, especially during the lockdown, but they never gave up on me. Thank you all very much.

I have used the word "Bombay" instead of "Mumbai" as it was called during my childhood. Similarly, I have used "Calcutta" instead of "Kolkata" for other cities.

At this stage of life, I have fulfilled my creative pursuit by writing. Perhaps, it's a new beginning for me as a writer...

About The Author

Shobha Srivastava has just celebrated her 80th birthday and while she completed her masters in Psychology almost 60 years back, she has remained a student of humanities all her life. Brought up in Jhansi and Mumbai, educated in Mumbai and Jabalpur, Shobha lived in various towns across the country before calling Pune her home.

Shobha is a voracious reader herself and in addition to being a very successful homemaker has dabbled in arts, crafts and the family business before retiring with her loving family by her side. In addition to reading, her interests include art and travel.

9 789358 195385

Printed by Libri Plureos GmbH in Hamburg,
Germany